The Book of
Great Funny One-liners

The Book of Great Funny One-liners

Frank Allen

NEW HOLLAND

First published in Australia in 2008 by
New Holland Publishers (Australia) Pty Ltd
Sydney • Auckland • London • Cape Town
1/66 Gibbes Street Chatswood NSW 2067 Australia
218 Lake Road Northcote Auckland New Zealand
86 Edgware Road London W2 2EA United Kingdom
80 McKenzie Street Cape Town 8001 South Africa

National Library of Australia Cataloguing-in-Publication Data:
Allen, Frank
Great funny one-liners Frank Allen.
            Wit and humor.
            Joking.
            Quotations, English.
            Invective--Humor.
            Invective--Quotations, maxims, etc.
            A808.882

ISBN: 9781741107005

Publisher: Fiona Schultz
Publishing Manager: Lliane Clarke
Project Editor: Christine Chua
Designer: Natasha Hayles
Production Assistant: Liz Malcolm
Printer: McPherson's Printing Group, Victoria

Contents

Introduction

In *Hamlet*, William Shakespeare wrote: 'Since brevity is the soul of wit, And tediousness the limbs and outward flourishes, I will be brief...'

And so I shall be.

The current incarnation of the succinct funny remark is the sound bite or grab—that short selection of words designed to give us the maximum amount of bang for the minimum amount of buck, or to give it another name, the one-liner.

In a world where we run the risk of suffocation in a blizzard of information it's nice to know that there have been many fine minds (and more than a few mediocre ones) who, in an idle moment, decided to spend their brain power on making themselves laugh, and us too, using just a few well-chosen (or unintentionally funny) words.

Herein I've gathered what I think are some pretty fine, short quotations that hit the nail right on the head without resorting to clichés. Use them to exercise your mind, to inspire you to come up with your own variations or steal them outright to cover up your own creative deficiencies, just like I have.

Goodness knows there are many occasions when we'd like to appear more scintillatingly witty than we usually are, so if you're looking for a juicy phrase or if you just want to have some fun, here they are. I hope you enjoy these great funny one-liners and have the opportunity to use one or two. Enjoy.

Frank Allen

It's Good to Be Bad

I am a drinker with a writing problem.

Brendan Behan, Irish dramatist

I've stopped drinking. But only while I'm asleep.

George Best, British soccer star

I've been told that alcohol is a slow poison. I'm in no hurry.

Robert Benchley, American humorist

I feel the end approaching. Quick! Bring my dessert, coffee and liqueur.

Jean Antheleme Brillat-Savarin, the French gastronome, on his deathbed

Who bothers to cook TV dinners? I suck them frozen.

Woody Allen, American film maker, comic and writer

I was eating a lot of frozen dinners when I realised they would probably taste better if they were warm.

Yakov Smirnoff, Ukrainian-American comedian

A nutrient is a chemical added to breakfast cereal to allow it to be sold as food.

Mike Barfield, American wit

I smoke ten to fifteen cigars a day. At my age I have to hold on to something.

George Burns, American comedian

I drink too much. The last time I gave a urine sample it had an olive in it.

Rodney Dangerfield, American comedian

I never drink because I was born intoxicated.

George Russell, American jazz pianist

Prohibition is better than no liquor at all.

Will Rogers, American humorist

The best way to cure a hangover is to avoid alcohol the night before.

Cathy Hopkins, British writer

There's nothing like good food, good wine and a bad girl.

Robin Williams, American actor and comedian

There is only one thing to be said in favour of drink and that is that it has caused many a lady to be loved that might have otherwise died single.

Finley Peter Dunne, American humorist

Have you heard about the Irishman who joined Alcoholics Anonymous? He still drinks, but under a different name.

Aubrey Dillon-Malone, British writer

The trouble with Italian food is that five or six days later you're hungry again.

George Miller, Australian film producer

I don't like people who take drugs—like customs officers for example.

Mick Miller, British comedian

It would be nice if the Food and Drug Administration stopped issuing warnings about toxic substances and just gave us the names of the one or two things still safe to eat.

Robert Fuoss, American writer

When I die they will write in the newspapers that the sons-of-bitches have lost their leader.

Vincent Gardenia, American actor

Princess Margaret is the Billy Carter of the British monarchy.

Robert Lacey, British biographer

At big dinners my motto always is 'Eat it now, you can always vomit it later'.

Derek Nimmo, British actor

The perfect lover is one who turns into a pizza at 4am.

Charles Pierce, American female impersonator

I slept like a baby. Every three hours I woke up looking for a bottle.

Liam O'Reilly, Irish musician

I phoned my dad to tell him I had stopped smoking. He called me a quitter.

Steven Pearl, American comic

It was a French physician, naturally enough, who first described the disease known as cirrhosis of the liver.

Richard Selzer, American surgeon and author

There are two things in life I like firm and one of them is jelly.

Mae West, American actor

I haven't touched a drop of alcohol since the invention of the funnel.

Malachy McCourt, Irish-American actor

Inhabitants of underdeveloped nations and victims of natural disasters are the only people who have ever been happy to see soya beans.

Fran Leibowitz, American wit

Never serve oysters in a month that has no pay check in it.

P.J. O'Rourke, American writer

After a good dinner, one can forgive anybody, even one's own relations.

Oscar Wilde, Irish playwright and wit

Spanish wine is foul. Cat piss is champagne compared to this sulphurous urination of some aged horse.

D.H. Lawrence, British writers

Making a Living

I am very fond of fresh air and royalties.
Daisy Ashford, English writer

Money is something that you have got to make in case you don't die.
Max Asnas, Russian-American restaurateur

It is better to give than to lend, and it costs about the same.
Philip Gibbs, English writer

Two can live as cheaply as one for half as long.
Howard Kandel, American writer

It is better to have a permanent income than to be fascinating.
Oscar Wilde, Irish playwright and wit

Anyone who lives within their means suffers from a lack of imagination.
Oscar Wilde, Irish playwright and wit

They were a people so primitive that they did not know how to get money except by working for it.
Joseph Addison, English essayist

An expert is someone who has made all the mistakes that can be made, but in a very narrow field.
Niels Bohr, Danish atomic physicist

They say it's better to be poor and happy than to be rich and miserable. But couldn't some compromise be worked out, like being moderately wealthy and just a little moody?

John Henry, American futures trader

I don't really have anything against work. I just figure, why deprive someone who really enjoys it?

American actor Dwayne Hickman in the role of Dobie Gillis

I don't know much about being a millionaire but I'll bet I'd be a darling at it.

Dorothy Parker, American journalist, writer and all-round wit

Whoever said money can't buy happiness simply hadn't found out where to go shopping.

Bo Derek, American actor

The world is filled with willing people; some willing to work, the rest willing to let them.

Robert Frost, American poet

The general advertiser's attitude would seem to be: if you are a lousy, smelly, idle, under-privileged, overweight and oversexed status-seeking moron, give me your money.

Kenneth Bromfield, American writer

I have never been in a situation where having money made it worse.

Clinton Jones, American footballer

When you've got them by their wallets, their hearts and minds will follow.

American wit Fern Naito famously paraphrased by Richard Nixon as 'If you've got them by the balls, their hearts and minds will follow.'

Lawyers, I suppose, were children once.

Charles Lamb, British essayist

I need enough to tide me over until I need more.

Bill Hoest, American cartoonist

Gentlemen prefer bonds.

Andrew Mellon, American banker

There is only one thing for a man to do who is married to a woman who enjoys spending money, and that is to enjoy earning it.

Edgar W. Howe, American editor and publisher

We don't just honour credit cards, we venerate them!

Dale McFeathers, American journalist

The only reason I made a commercial for American Express is to pay for my American Express bill.

Peter Ustinov, British comedian and actor

You can't pay your Visa on your American Express card.

P.J. O'Rourke, American writer

Historians are like deaf people who go on answering questions no-one has asked them.

Leo Tolstoy, Russian novelist

Consultants are people who borrow your watch to tell you what time it is and then walk off with it.

Robert Townsend, American actor

I don't like work even when someone else does it.

Mark Twain, American writer

In spite of the cost of living, it's still popular.

Kathleen Norris, American novelist

Part of the $10 million I spent on gambling, part on booze and part on women. The rest I spent foolishly.

George Raft, American actor

A bargain is something you can't use at a price you can't resist.

Franklin P. Jones, American writer

We don't seem to be able to check crime, so why not legalise it and tax it out of business?

Will Rogers, American humorist

Unquestioningly there is progress. The average American now pays out twice as much in taxes as he formerly got in wages.

H.L. Mencken, American journalist and political commentator

Few great men would have got past Personnel.

Paul Goodman, American writer

The trouble with unemployment is that the minute you wake up in the morning, you're on the job.

Lena Horne, American singer

Men on Men and Women

My wife finds it hard to envision me as the end product of millions of years of evolution.

Bob Barnes, American cartoonist

I don't know the question, but sex is definitely the answer.

American film maker, comic and writer Woody Allen

There is at least one fool in every married couple.

Henry Fielding, British novelist and dramatist

Is sex dirty? Only if it's done right.

American film maker, comic and writer Woody Allen

Of all my wife's relations I like myself the best.

Joe Cook, American actor

Brigands demand your money or your life—women require both.

Samuel Butler, British writer

A woman's preaching is like a dog's walking on his hinder legs. It is not done well; but you are surprised to find it done at all.

British writer Samuel Johnson, as quoted by his biographer, James Boswell

The secret of a successful marriage is not to be at home too much.

Colin Chapman, British designer

In my house I'm the boss. My wife is just the decision maker.

American film maker, comic and writer Woody Allen

In India a farmhand was caught in the act with his cow. He said he had bad eyesight and thought it was his wife.

Spike Milligan, British actor and comedian

They kept mistresses of such dowdiness they might almost have been mistaken for wives.

Roberston Davies, American writer

An appropriate age for marriage is 18 for girls and 37 for men.

Aristotle, ancient Greek philosopher

If thee marries for money, thee surely will earn it.

Ezra Bowen, American editor

Housework is what a woman does that nobody notices until she hasn't done it.

Evan Esar, American humorist

There is little wife-swapping in suburbia. It is unnecessary, the females all being so similar.

Richard Gordon, British broadcaster

Have I ever paid for sex? Only emotionally.

Lee Hurst, British comedian

Don't knock masturbation. It's sex with someone you love.

Woody Allen, American film maker, comic and writer

When authorities warn you of the dangers of sex, there is an important lesson to be learned. Do not have sex with the authorities.

Matt Groening, American cartoonist and creator of *The Simpsons*

You're getting old if you discuss the facts of life with your children and you get slapped by your wife when you attempt to try out some of the things they told you.

Russell Bell, American actor

To please my wife, I decided to get in touch with my feminine side. Now I've got a yeast infection.

Bob Delaney, American basketball referee

Everyone should be married. A bachelor's life is no life for a single man.

Samuel Goldwyn, American film studio director

The three words you don't want to hear while making love are 'Honey, I'm home'.

Ken Hammond, Canadian hockey player

I'm glad I'm not bisexual. I couldn't stand being rejected by men as well as women.

Bernard Manning, British comedian

'Tis better to have loved and lost than never to have lost at all.

Samuel Butler, British writer

Remember men, we're fighting for this woman's honour, which is more than she ever did.

Groucho Marx, American actor and comedian

You're getting old when the girl you smile at thinks you're one of her father's friends.

Arthur Murray, American dance impresario

Sex is one of the most wholesome, beautiful things money can buy.

Steve Martin, American comedian

I will not allow my daughters to learn foreign languages because one tongue is sufficient for a woman.

John Milton, British poet

The best way to remember your wife's birthday is to forget it once.

Joseph Cossman, American entrepreneur

I wouldn't be caught dead marrying a woman old enough to be my wife.

Tony Curtis, American actor

My wife's hands are so beautiful I'm going to have a bust made of them.

Samuel Goldwyn, American film studio director

Women are called the opposite sex because when you want to do anything they want to do the opposite.

Corey Ford, American humorist

I asked her if she was doing anything on Saturday night and she told me she was committing suicide. So I asked her if she was doing anything on Friday night.

Woody Allen, American film maker, comic and writer

Under 21 women are protected by law; over 65 they're protected by nature; anything in between is fair game.

Cary Grant, American actor

Women run everything. The only thing I have decided in my house over the last twenty years is to recognise Angola as an independent state.

Brian Clough, British footballer

It's hard to lose a mother-in-law. In fact, it's almost impossible.

W.C. Fields, American actor

The Grand Canyon—what a marvellous place to drop one's mother-in-law.

Ferdinand Foch, French soldier

I'm not a breast man. I'm a breast person.

John Wilson, British writer

We have a saying in Russia, 'Women are like buses.' That's it.

Yakov Smirnoff, Ukranian-American comedian

God made Adam before Eve because he didn't want any advice on the matter.

Patrick Murray, British actor

Women on Women and Men

When I eventually met Mr Right, I had no idea his first name was 'Always'.

Rita Rudner, American comedian

Men carry their brains lower than women do, so when they're scratching their crotches they're not being gross—they're just thinking.

Diana Jordan, American comedian

Men should be like Kleenex—soft, strong and disposable.

Cher, American singer and actor

The only reason I would take up jogging is so I could hear heavy breathing again.

Erma Bombeck, American humorist

My true friends have always given me that supreme proof of devotion; a spontaneous aversion for the man I loved.

Colette, French author

I believe in large families; everyone should have at least three husbands.

Zsa Zsa Gabor, Hungarian-American actor

Never trust a man with testicles.

The useless piece of flesh at the end of a man's penis is called the man.

Jo Brand, British comedian

Men aren't attracted to me by my mind. They are attracted to me by what I don't mind.

Gypsy Rose Lee, American stripper

Every woman needs at least three men: one for sex, one for money and one for fun.

Bess Myerson, first Jewish woman to win the Miss America Pageant (1945)

A sexagenarian! At his age! I think that's disgusting.

Gracie Allen, American comedian

There is so little difference between husbands that you might as well keep the first.

Adela Rogers Saint-Johns, American writer

Give a man a free hand and he'll run it all over you.

Mae West, American actor

Men have simple needs. They can survive the whole weekend with only three things—beer, boxer shorts and batteries for the remote control.

Diana Jordan, American comedian

My mother-in-law is so fat, she has her own ZIP code.

Phyllis Diller, American comedian

I love men, not because they are men, but because they are not women.

Queen Christina of Sweden

Beware of the man who picks your dresses; he wants to wear them.

Erica Jong, American author

She would be a nymphomaniac if they could only calm her down a little.

Judy Garland, American singer and actor

Never marry a man with a big head, because you're going to give birth to that man's child and you want a baby with a narrow head.

Jilly Goolden, British media personality

Sleeping with Aldous Huxley was like being crawled over by slugs.

Nancy Cunard, American socialite

When a man makes a woman his wife, it's the highest compliment he can pay her, and it's usually the last.

Helen Rowland, American journalist

Whatever else can be said about sex, it cannot be called a dignified performance.

Helen Lawrenson, American journalist

Men and Women on Boys and Girls

I don't want to adopt. Not with my genes. I have award-winning genes.

Woody Allen, American film maker, comic and writer

When you are eight years old, nothing is any of your business.

Lenny Bruce, American comedian

Tired mothers find that spanking takes less time than reasoning and penetrates sooner to the seat of memory.

Will Durant, American historian

Madam, there's no such thing as a tough child—if you boil them first for a few hours, they always come out tender.

W.C. Fields, American actor

As a housewife, I feel that if the kids are still alive when my husband comes home from work, then hey, I've done my job.

Roseanne Barr, American comedian

Insanity is hereditary. You can catch it from your kids.

Erma Bombeck, American humorist

Don't bother discussing sex with small children. They rarely have anything to add.

Fran Leibowitz, American wit

One thing they never tell you about child raising is that for the rest of your life, at the drop of a hat, you are expected to know your child's name and how old he or she is.

Erma Bombeck, American humorist

Try flying in a plane with a baby if you want a sense of what it must have been like to be a leper in the fourteenth century.

Nora Ephron, American film director

There are few things more satisfying than seeing your children have teenagers of their own.

Doug Larson, British racer

The worst eternal triangle known is: teenager, parent and telephone.

Lavonne Mathison, American writer

My schooldays were the happiest days of my life—which gives you some idea of the misery I've endured over the past twenty-five years.

Paul Merton, British actor

We had bad luck with our kids—they all grew up.

Christopher Morley, American editor and author

Never underestimate a child's ability to get into more trouble.

Martin Mull, American actor

I decided to have a vasectomy after a family vote on the matter. The kids voted for it eleven to three.

Brendan O'Carroll, Irish comedian

In general, my children refused to eat anything that hadn't danced on TV.

Erma Bombeck, American humorist

The only sense I can make out of having kids is that it's a good way to become a grandparent.

Ralph Noble, American writer

Even young children need to be informed about dying. Explain the concept of death very carefully to your child. This will make threatening him with it much more effective.

P.J. O'Rourke, American writer

Don't have sex, man. It leads to kissing and pretty soon you have to talk to them.

Steve Martin, American comedian

God invented vegetables to let women get even with their children.

P.J. O'Rourke, American writer

Heredity is what sets the parents of a teenager wondering about each other.

Lawrence J. Peter, American writer famous for The Peter Principle, the management 'law' that states that everyone is promoted up to the point where they reach their level of incompetence.

I never want to become pregnant, ever. To me life is hard enough without having someone kick you from the inside.

Rita Rudner, American comedian

No matter how old a mother is, she watches her middle-aged children for signs of improvement.

Florida Scott-Maxwell, American journalist

One of my school reports read as follows—'This boy shows great originality, which must be crushed at all costs'.

Peter Ustinov, British comedian and actor

My teenage son is half-man, half-mattress.

Val Valentine, British screenwriter

The main purpose of children's parties is to remind you that there are children worse than your own.

Katherine Whitehorn, British journalist

Parents are not interested in justice; they are interested in peace and quiet.

Bill Cosby, American comedian

Babies don't need a vacation but I still see them at the beach. I'll go over to a little baby and say, 'What are you doing here? You've never worked a day in your life.'

Steven Wright, American comedian

To lose one parent, Mr Worthing, may be regarded as a misfortune; to lose both looks like carelessness.

Oscar Wilde, Irish playwright and wit

My unhealthy affection for my second daughter has waned. I now despise all of my seven children equally.

Evelyn Waugh, British novelist

The Body Beautiful

I can never understand why, when I was born, I was the one who ended up with the stretch marks.

Linda Agran, American producer

She wore a low but futile décolletage.

Dorothy Parker, American writer and poet

My photographs don't do me justice—they look just like me.

Phyllis Diller, American comedian

Women complain about premenstrual syndrome. But I think of it as the only time of the month I can be myself.

Roseanne Barr, American comedian

Women should try to increase their size rather than to decrease it, because I believe the bigger we are, the more space we'll take up, and the more we'll have to be reckoned with.

Roseanne Barr, American comedian

When I go to the beauty parlour, I always use the emergency entrance. Sometimes I just go for an estimate.

Phyllis Diller, American comedian

Of course William Morris was a wonderful artist and an all-round man, but the art of walking round him always made me tired.

Max Beerbohm, British caricaturist

Seize the moment. Think of all those women on the *Titanic* who waved off the dessert cart.

Erma Bombeck, American humorist

He's so fat, he can be his own running mate.

Johnny Carson, American television presenter

You couldn't tell if she was dressed for an opera or an operation.

Irvin S. Cobb, American writer

Think of me as a sex symbol who doesn't give a damn.

Phyllis Diller, American comedian

If her dress had pockets my wife would look like a pool table.

Rodney Dangerfield, American comedian

I'm so fat that when I get my shoes cleaned, I have to take the shoeshine's word for it.

Stubby Kaye, American comic actor

She could very well pass for forty-three. In the dusk with the light behind her.

W.S. Gilbert, British librettist

Take those scales out of the bathroom; the right place for them is in front of the refrigerator.

Richard Needham, British politician

The tautness of his face sours ripe grapes.

William Shakespeare, British dramatist

A four-hundred-dollar suit on him would look like socks on a rooster.

American politician Earl Long on an anonymous rival

My mother-in-law's face is her fortune. She pays no income tax.

Les Dawson, British comedian

Handsome? He looked like a dog's bum with a hat on.

Spike Milligan, British actor and comedian

Outside every thin woman is a fat woman dying to get in.

Katherine Whitehorn, British journalist

I have no boobs whatsoever. On my wedding night my husband said, 'Let me help you with those buttons' and I told him, 'I'm completely naked.'

Joan Rivers, American comedian

God knew from all eternity that I was going to be Pope. You think he would have made me more photogenic.

Pope John XXIII

Why don't you get a haircut? You look like a chrysanthemum.

P.G. Wodehouse, British writer

She is a peacock in everything but beauty.

Oscar Wilde, Irish playwright and wit

Foreigners and Their Parts

When asked by an anthropologist what the Indians called America before the white man came, an Indian simply said 'Ours'.

Vine Deloria, American anthropologist

America is a society which believes that God is dead but Elvis is alive.

Irving Kupcinet, American columnist

It is by the goodness of God that in our country we have those three unspeakably precious things: freedom of speech, freedom of conscience, and the prudence to never practice either of them.

Mark Twain, American writer

I went to join the New York public library. The guy told me I had to prove I was a citizen of New York, so I stabbed him.

Emo Philips, American comedian

There won't be any revolution in America... the people are too clean. They spend all their time changing their shirts and washing themselves. You can't feel fierce and revolutionary in a bathroom.

Eric Linklater, British writer

Britain has invented a new missile. It's called the civil servant—it doesn't work and it can't be fired.

Walter Walker, British general

Canada could have enjoyed English government, French culture and American know-how. Instead it ended up with English know-how, French government and American culture.

John Robert Columbo, Canadian poet

The softer the currency in a foreign country, the harder the toilet paper.

John Fountain, American writer

The English winter—ending in July, to recommence in August.

George Gordon, British academic

The only pleasure an Englishman has is in passing on his cold germs.

Gerald Durrell, British author

I like the English. The English may not like music, but they absolutely love the noise it makes.

Thomas Beecham, British conductor

Those comfortably padded lunatic asylums which are known, euphemistically, as the stately homes of England.

Virginia Woolf, British writer

The English never smash in a face. They merely refrain from asking it to dinner.

Margaret Halsey, American writer

Foreigners and their Parts

British education is probably the best in the world, if you can survive it. If you can't there is nothing left for you but the diplomatic corps.

Peter Ustinov, British comedian and actor

The English people on the whole are surely the nicest people in the world, and everybody makes everything so easy for everyone else, that there is almost nothing to resist at all.

D. H. Lawrence, British author

It is no longer true that Continentals have a sex life whereas the English have hot water bottles—the English now have electric blankets.

George Mikes, Hungarian-British writer

Much may be made of a Scotchman, if he be caught young.

Samuel Johnson, English writer and lexicographer

I have been trying all my life to like Scotsmen, and am obliged to desist from the experiment in despair.

Charles Lamb, English essayist

The Irish climate is wonderful, but the weather ruins it.

Tony Butler, British sports broadcaster

If one could teach the English to talk and the Irish to listen, society would be quite civilised.

Oscar Wilde, Irish playwright and wit

The French don't care what they do as long as they pronounce it properly.

George Bernard Shaw, Irish playwright

When St Patrick first visited Ireland there was no word in the Irish language to express sobriety.

Oliver St John Gogarty, Irish physician

Given the unlikely options of attending a funeral or a sex orgy, a true Irishman will always opt for the funeral.

John B. Keane, Irish writer

A complete description of Belfast is given by: population 200,000; early closing day Wednesday.

Shamus O'Shamus, Irish comedian

Heaven is an English policeman, a French cook, a German engineer, an Italian lover and everything organised by the Swiss. Hell is an English cook, a French engineer, a German policeman, a Swiss lover and everything organised by the Italians.

John Elliot, American songwriter

The Swiss are not so much a people as a neat, clean, quite solvent business.

William Faulkner, American novelist

We had a very successful trip to Russia—we got back.

Bob Hope, American comedian

An Iranian moderate is one who has run out of ammunition.

Henry Kissinger, German-American politician

Germans are flummoxed by humour, the Swiss have no concept of fun, the Spanish think there is nothing at all ridiculous about eating dinner at midnight, and the Italians should never, ever have been let in on the invention of the motor car.

Bill Bryson, American author

I do not see the EEC as a great love affair. It is more like nine middle-aged couples with failing marriages meeting at a Brussels hotel for a group grope.

Kenneth Tynan, British writer

The high standards of Australians are due to the fact that their ancestors were all handpicked by the best English judges.

Douglas Copeland, Canadian novelist

There are only two classes of persons in New South Wales—those who have been convicted and those who ought to have been.

Lachlan Macquarie, governor of the colony of New South Wales

Many people are surprised to hear we have comedians in Russia, but there they are. They are dead, but there they are.

'Vacation' is the word Americans use to describe going someplace different to have fun and get away from all their trials and tribulations. The English call it 'holiday'. In Russia it's known as 'defecting'.

Yakov Smirnoff, Ukranian-American comedian

Human by
Correspondence

A conservative government is an organised hypocrisy.

Benjamin Disraeli, British statesman

If Gladstone fell into the Thames, that would be a misfortune, and if anybody pulled him out of that, I suppose, would be a calamity.

Benjamin Disraeli on fellow British Prime Minister William Gladstone

He is a self-made man and worships his creator.

British statesman John Bright on Benjamin Disraeli

He never spares himself in conversation. He gives himself so generously that hardly anyone else is permitted to give anything in his presence.

British politician Aneurin Bevan on Winston Churchill

Aneurin Bevan is a thrombosis. A bloody clot that undermines the constitution.

Winston Churchill, British statesman

The Prime Minister has an absolute genius for putting flamboyant labels on empty luggage.

British politician Aneurin Bevan on Harold Macmillan

Giving money and power to the government is like giving whiskey and car keys to teenage boys.

P.J. O'Rourke, American writer

Tony Blair has pushed moderation to extremes.

Robert MacLennan, Scottish politician

This island is made mainly of coal and is surrounded by fish. Only an organising genius could produce a shortage of coal and fish at the same time.

British politician Aneurin Bevan on the Tory Party

It was said Mr Gladstone could convince most people of most things, and himself of anything.

British clergyman Dean William R. Inge on William Gladstone

Aneurin Bevan of course was himself far from being universally admired. He even felt the betrayal of his own Labour Party exclaiming once to them: 'Damn it all, you can't have the crown of thorns and the thirty pieces of silver!'

Daily Express comment on Bevan

My colleagues tell military secrets to their wives, except Asquith who tells them to other people's wives.

Lord Kitchener (the model for the famous and oft-imitated *I Want You* poster of WWI).

We'd all like to vote for the best man but he's never a candidate.

Kin Hubbard, American cartoonist and humorist

Winston is always expecting rabbits to come out of empty hats.

Field Marshall Lord Waveil on Winston Churchill's handling of WWII

The Honourable Gentleman should not generate more indignation than he can conveniently contain.

Winston Churchill to an overly irate politician William Wedgwood Benn

I have a great admiration for Mussolini, who has welded a nation out of a collection of touts, blackmailers, ice-cream vendors and gangsters.

Michael Bateman, British journalist

If Max gets to Heaven he won't last long. He will be chucked out for trying to pull off a merger between Heaven and Hell... after having secured a controlling interest in key subsidiary companies in both places, of course.

Briish writer H.G. Wells on Lord Beaverbrook.

His ear is so sensitively attuned to the bugle note of history that he is often deaf to the more raucous clamour of modern life.

British Labour politician Aneurin Bevan on Winston Churchill

John Major is the only man who ran away from the circus to become an accountant.

Edward Pearce, British writer

When you have a skunk it is better to have him inside the tent pissing out than outside pissing in.

President Lyndon B. Johnson on J. Edgar Hoover

Harold Wilson is going around the country stirring up apathy.

William Whitelaw, British politician

The best description of Margaret Thatcher I ever heard is that she's just the sort of woman who wouldn't give you your ball back.

Mike Harding, British comedian

Trust J. Edgar Hoover as much as you would a rattlesnake with a silencer on his rattle.

Dean Acheson. American statesman

A fool and his money are soon elected.

Will Rogers, American humorist

Rumsfeld is admired as a genius by people who find conceit alone to be evidence of genius.

Beast magazine's description of Donald Rumsfeld

Politics is derived from two words—poly, meaning many, and tics, meaning small, blood-sucking insects.

Chris Clayton, American writer

Ambassador, n. A person who, having failed to secure an office from the people, is given one by the administration on the condition that he leaves the country.

Ambrose Bierce, American writer

A statesman is a dead politician. We need more statesmen.

Bob Edwards, American radio host

Nixon impeached himself. He gave us Gerald Ford as revenge.

Bella Abzug, American feminist

A year ago Gerald Ford was unknown around the country. Now he's unknown throughout the world.

Norman Mailer, American writer

Most politicians look like people who have become human by correspondence course.

A.A. Gill, British columnist

Some Republicans are so ignorant that they wouldn't know how to pour piss out of a boot—even if the instructions were written on the heel.

Lyndon B. Johnson, American president

One could drive a schooner through any part of his argument and never scrape against a fact.

David Houston on fellow American politician William Jennings Bryan

As an intellectual he bestowed upon the games of golf and bridge all the enthusiasm and perseverance that he withheld from books and ideas.

American writer Emmet Hughes on Dwight Eisenhower

To err is Truman.

Walter Winchell, American commentator

All political parties die at last from swallowing their own lies.

John Arbuthnot, Scottish writer and physician

Mr Howard and his government are just Yes-men to the United States. There they are, a conga line of suckholes on the conservative side of Australian politics.

Australian politician Mark Latham on John Howard

In Pierre Trudeau Canada has at last produced a politician worthy of assassination.

Irving Layton, Canadian poet

Under democracy one party always devotes its chief energies to trying to prove that the other party is unfit to rule, and both commonly succeed, and are right.

H. L. Mencken, American journalist

There are two politicians drowning and you are allowed to save only one. What do you do? Read a newspaper or eat your lunch?

Mort Sahl, American comedian

If there had been any formidable body of cannibals in the country he would have promised to provide them with free missionaries, fattened at the taxpayer's expense.

American journalist H.L. Mencken on Harry Truman's 1948 presidential campaign

Asked if they'd have sex with President Clinton, 90 per cent of American women replied 'Never again.'

Albert Roge, American writer

A semi-housetrained polecat.

Michael Foot on Norman Tebbit

Bill Clinton is the only politician in the world who can distract people's attention from one sex scandal by being involved in another.

Matthew Campbell, Australian footballer

If he became convinced tomorrow that coming out for cannibalism would get him the votes he surely needs, he would begin fattening a missionary in the White House backyard come Wednesday.

American journalist H.L. Mencken on president Franklin D. Roosevelt

When German-American politician Henry Kissinger won the Nobel Peace Prize, I gave up satire on the grounds of unfair competition.

Tom Lehrer, American musical satirist

Politics is show business for ugly people.

Paul Begala, American political consultant

I've noticed that everyone who is for abortion has already been born.

Ronald Reagan, American president

Politicians are like nappies. They should be changed regularly and for the same reason.

Patrick Murray, Britsh actor

Politicians are people who, when they see light at the end of the tunnel, order more tunnel.

John Quintan, British commentator

Self-esteem is a good thing but anyone who has ever toilet trained a child knows that it is possible to make too much of the efforts of the child on the potty. One wonders if little Ed Koch was told once too often what a great thing he'd done and began to think that all that emanated from his being was pretty great.

Peggy Noonan. American writer

Washington couldn't tell a lie, Nixon couldn't tell the truth and Reagan couldn't tell the difference.

Mort Sahl, American comedian

There are only a few original jokes and most of them are in Congress.

Will Rogers, American humorist

Theodore Roosevelt was an old maid with testosterone poisoning.

Patricia O'Toole, American writer

John Tyler has been called a mediocre man; but this is unwarranted flattery. He was a man of monumental littleness.

Theodore Roosevelt, American president

I fired Douglas McArthur because he wouldn't respect the office of the President. I didn't fire him because he was a dumb son of a bitch, although he was.

Harry S. Truman, American president

Arthur Scargill couldn't negotiate his way out of a toilet.

Ray Lynk, American businessman

Never in the history of fashion has so little material been raised so high to reveal so much that needs to be covered so badly.
Cecil Beaton, British photographer

The news of President Eisenhower's campaigning for Richard Nixon depresses me. After a clear record of eight years, I hate to see him involved in politics.
Mort Sahl, American comedian

I have nothing against Nicholas Ridley's wife or family, but I think it's time he spent more time with them.
Philip Goodhart, British politician

Congressmen are so damned dumb, they could throw themselves on the ground and miss.
James Traficant, American politician

Dan Quayle taught the kids a valuable lesson: if you don't study you could end up Vice-President.
Jay Leno, American television presenter

I never accepted a knighthood because to me honour is enough. Besides, they get one into disreputable company.
George Bernard Shaw, Irish playwright

Quoting Ronald Reagan accurately is called mud slinging.
Walter Mondale, American vice president

The illegitimate child of Karl Marx and Catherine the Great.
Clement Atlee on Russian communism

As for the look on Dan Quayle's face—how to describe it? If a tree fell in a forest, and there was no one to hear it, it might sound like Dan Quayle looks.

Tom Shales, American critic

A British prime minister was on a tour of New York when his proud guide pointed out a building that was so solid that it would last a thousand years.

'Dear, dear me! What a pity!' he replied.

The President is going to lead us out of this recovery.

Dan Quayle, American vice president

Poor George. He can't help it. He was born with a silver foot in his mouth.

Ann Richards, former Governor of Texas

George Bush's problem is that the clothes have no emperor.

Anna Quindlen, American writer

Paul Shannon is educated beyond his intelligence.

Dennis Skinner, British politician

You have to get to know Dewey to dislike him.

Robert A. Taft, American politician

They inculcate the morals of a whore and the manners of a dancing master.

Samuel Johnson, English writer and lexicographer, on Lord Chesterfield's letters of advice to his son

Democracy is a pathetic belief in the collective wisdom of individual ignorance.

H.L. Mencken, American journalist and political commentator

Margaret Beckett looks like a woman resigned to walk home alone to an empty bed-sit after Grab-a-Granny night at the local disco.

Richard Littlejohn, British writer

The idea of Prince Charles conversing with vegetables is not quite so amusing when you remember that he's had plenty of practice chatting to members of his own family.

Jaci Stephens, British journalist

Eyesores and Sore Eyes

What is art? Prostitution.

Charles Baudelaire, French writer

It makes me look as if I were straining a stool.

Winston Churchill commenting on his famous portrait by Graham Sutherland

A decorator tainted with insanity.

American art critic Kenyon Cox on Paul Gauguin

When I see a man of shallow understanding extravagantly clothed, I feel sorry—for the clothes.

Josh Billings, American humorist

Mona Lisa looks as if she has just been sick or is about to be.

Noel Coward, British actor and dramatist

A living is made by selling something everybody needs at least once a year. And a million is made by producing something that everybody needs every day. You artists produce something nobody needs at any time.

Thornton Wilder, American playwright

I am the only woman in the world who had had her dresses rejected by the Salvation Army.

Phyllis Diller, American comedian

Saint Laurent has excellent taste. The more he copies me, the better taste he displays.

Coo Chanel on fellow French couturier Yves Saint Laurent

I wouldn't have that hanging in my home. It would be like living with a gas leak.

Dame Edith Evans, British actor

Another word from you, and I'll paint you as you are!

A frustrated German artist Max Leiberman to a sitter who wouldn't shut up

I am lonesome. They are all dying. I have hardly a warm personal enemy left.

James McNeill Whistler, American painter

The murals in restaurants are about on par with the food in art galleries.

Peter de Vries, American editor

The goitrous, torpid and squinting husks provided by Matisse in his sculpture are worthless except as tactful decorations for a mental home.

Percy Wyndham-Lewis, Canadian-British painter

Fashion is a form of ugliness so intolerable that we have to alter it every six months.

Oscar Wilde, Irish playwright and wit

Your right to wear a mint-green polyester leisure suit ends where it meets my eyes.

Fran Leibowitz, American wit

Eyesores and Sore Eyes

Movers, Warblers and Other Noise Makers

Far too noisy, my dear Mozart, far too many notes…

Archduke Ferdinand of Austria on Wolfgang Amadeus Mozart

For three hundred years flautists tried to play in tune. Then they gave up and invented vibrato.

George Barrere, French flautist

An ambulatory hamburger.

Beast magazine's description of US country and western singer Toby Keith

When an opera star sings her head off, she usually improves her appearance.

Victor Borge, Danish-American humorist and musician

The world we live in is in a funny state. Someone goes out and shoots John Lennon and lets Des O'Connor live.

Roy Brown, British comedian

This man forgot how to sound or look natural thirty years ago.

British journalist Dave Jennings on British singer Cliff Richard

A glorified bandmaster.

British composer Thomas Beecham on Italian composer Arturo Toscanini

The true gentleman is a man who knows how to play the bagpipes but doesn't.

British composer Thomas Beecham on fellow British composer Edward Elgar

British conductor Thomas Beecham was a pompous little band master who stood against anything creative in the art of his time.

John Fowles, British novelist

Sleep is an excellent way of listening to an opera.

James Stephens, critic

Liszt's bombast is bad; it is very bad; in fact there is only one thing worse in his music, and that is his affected and false simplicity. It was said of George Sand that she had a habit of speaking and writing concerning chastity in such terms that the very word became impure; so it is with the simplicity of Liszt.

American critic Philip Hale on Hungarian composer Franz Liszt

Perhaps it was because Nero played the fiddle, they burned Rome.

Oliver Herford, American writer

Modern music is just noise with attitude.

Patrick Murray, British actor

Liszt's so-called piano music is nothing but Chopin and brandy.

James Huneker, American music critic

How could I possibly have a sexual relationship with a fifty-year-old fossil? I have a beautiful boyfriend of twenty-eight. Why should I swap for a dinosaur?

Italian singer and model Carla Bruni on Mick Jagger. Bruni has nevertheless dated Eric Clapton, Kevin Costner and Donald Trump, and in 2008 married 53-year-old French president Nicolas Sarkozy

This man has child-bearing lips.

American comedian Joan Rivers on Mick Jagger

I don't understand anything about the ballet. All I know is that during the intervals the ballerinas stink like horses.

Anton Chekov, Russian playwright

Splitting the convulsively inflated larynx of the Muse, Berg utters tortured mistuned cackling, a pandemonium of chopped-up orchestral sounds, mishandled men's throats, bestial outcries, bellowing, rattling, and all other evil noises... Berg is the poisoner of the well of German music.

German review of Austrian composer Alban Berg

He has Van Gogh's ear for music.

Billy Wilder, American film director

Berlioz composes by splashing his pen over the manuscript and leaving the issue to chance.

Polish composer Frederic Chopin on French composer Hector Berlioz

The tuba is certainly the most intestinal of instruments, the very lower bowel of music.

Peter de Vries, American editor

I can compare *Le Carnival Romain* by Berlioz to nothing but the caperings and gibberings of a big baboon, over-excited by a dose of alcoholic stimulus.

George Templeton Strong, British critic

Of all the bulls that live, this hath the greatest ass's ears.

Elizabeth I on John Bull

He was ignored till he began to smash the parlour furniture, throw bombs and hitch together ten pianolas, all playing different tunes, whereupon everyone began to talk about him.

American music critic Henry T. Fink on Austrian-American composer Arnold Schoenberg

Rock is a little boy's playground and little boys don't talk about anything that women are interested in or concerned about. Apart from how big their willies are.

Joe Fuzzbox, British writer

Jazz has a bad name because some of it is crap, and it's boring.

Jools Holland, British musician

Madonna is so hairy—when she lifted up her arm, I thought it was Tina Turner in her armpit.

Joan Rivers, American comedian

Take a look at Keith Richard's face. He's turned into leather. He's a giant suitcase. He has a handle on his head. That's how they move him around at concerts.

Denis Leary, American comedian

Movers, Warblers and Other Noise Makers

The reason I drink is because when I'm sober I think I'm Eddie Fisher.

Dean Martin, American singer and actor

I never watch the *Dinah Shore Show*—I'm a diabetic.

Oscar Levant, American musician and wit

His wantonness is not vicious. It is that of a great baby, rather tirelessly addicted to dressing himself up as Handel or Beethoven and making a prolonged and intolerable noise.

George Bernard Shaw, Irish playwright on Johannes Brahms

Brassy, brazen witch on a mortgaged broomstick, a steamroller with cleats.

Broadway theatre critic Walter Kerr on American singer and actor Ethel Merman

The audience seemed rather disappointed: they expected the ocean, something big, something colossal, but they were served instead with some agitated water in a saucer.

Critic Louis Schneider on *La Mer* by French composer Claude Debussy

Of all the bête, clumsy, blundering, boggling, baboon-blooded stuff that I ever saw on a human stage, that last night beat as far as the story and acting went all the affected, sapless, soulless, beginningless, endless, topless, bottomless, topsiturviest, tuneless, scrabble-pipiest-tongs and boniest-doggerel of sounds I ever endured the deadliness of, that eternity of nothing was deadliest, as far as its sound went.

British essayist John Ruskin on Richard Wagner

I liked the bit about quarter to eleven.

French composer Erik Satie on *La Mer* by French composer Claude Debussy

He sang like a hinge.

American singer and actor Ethel Merman on American composer Cole Porter

The concert is a polite form of self-imposed torture.

Henry Miller, American writer

… all England needs—another queen who can't dress.

American comedian Joan Rivers on British singer Boy George

If there is music in hell it will be bagpipes.

Joe Tomelty, British writer

His vibrato sounded like he was driving a tractor over ploughed fields with weights tied to his scrotum.

Spike Milligan, British actor and comedian

If I found her floating in my pool, I'd punish my dog.

American comedian Joan Rivers on Japanese-American artist Yoko Ono

Her voice sounded like an eagle being goosed.

American critic Ralph Novak on Yoko Ono

A provincial Debussy.

British historian A. J. P. Taylor on Frederick Delius

Waldo is one of those people who would be enormously improved by death.

British writer H.H. Munro, better known as Saki

Some people exist who like to see their names in print. John Lennon and Yoko Ono are print junkies.

Germaine Greer, Australian feminist

Rachmaninov's immortalising totality was his scowl. He was a six and a half foot scowl.

Igor Stravinsky on fellow Russian composer Sergei Rachmaninov

The musical equivalent of blancmange.

Journalist Bernard Levin on the work of fellow Brit, the composer Frederick Delius

Spinning Wheel, by Blood, Sweat and Tears, is music to commit voluntary euthanasia by.

Simon Hoggart, British journalist

The chief objection to playing wind instruments is that it prolongs the life of the player.

George Bernard Shaw, Irish playwright

Schoenberg would be better off shovelling snow.

German composer Richard Strauss on Austrian-Hungarian composer Arnold Schoenberg

I've always said that there's a place for the press but they haven't dug it yet.

Tommy Docherty, Scottish footballer

This is the best book ever written by any man on the wrong side of a question of which he was profoundly ignorant.

Thomas B. Macaulay, British essayist

Mr Robin Day asks me to vouch for the fact that he can sing. I testify that the noise he makes is in fact something between that of a cat drowning, a lavatory flushing and a hyena devouring her after birth in the Appalachian Mountains under a full moon.

British writer Auberon Waugh on the British political broadcaster

The approach of Frankie Lane to the microphone is that of an accused man pleading with a hostile jury.

Kenneth Tynan, British writer

After Rossini dies, who will there be to promote his music?

German composer Richard Wagner on Italian composer Gioacchino Rossini

Madam, I have cried only twice in my life; once when I dropped a wing of truffled chicken into Lake Como, and once for the first time I heard you sing.

Gioacchino Rossini, Italian composer

He is to piano playing as David Soul is to acting; he makes Jacques Loussier sound like Bach; he reminds us how cheap potent music can be.

Welsh conductor Richard Williams on French pianist Richard Clayderman

With regard to Gounod's *Redemption*, if you will only take the precaution to go in long enough after it commences and to come out long enough before it is over, you will not find it wearisome.

George Bernard Shaw, Irish playwright

Penners and Inkers

No poet or novelist wishes he were the only one who ever lived but most of them wish they were the only one alive and quite a few fondly believe their wish has been granted.

W.H. Auden, British writer

I read the newspapers avidly. It is my one form of continuous fiction.

Aneurin Bevan, British politician

Journalists are people who take in other people's washing and then sell it.

Marjorie Barnard and Flora Eldershaw, Australian writing team

Studying literature at Harvard is like learning about women at the Mayo Clinic.

Roy Blount, American writer

Carlyle is a poet to whom nature has denied the faculty of verse.

British poet Alfred, Lord Tennyson on Scottish essayist Thomas Carlyle

Sitting in a sewer and adding to it.

Scottish essayist Thomas Carlyle describing the poetry of Algernon Swinburne.

He not only overfilled with learning but stood in the slop.

Scottish writer Thomas Carlyle on British writer Thomas Babington Macaulay

I did so enjoy your book, darling. Everything that everybody writes in it is so good.

Mrs Patrick Campbell, British actor

Standing up to his neck in a cesspool and adding to its contents.

American poet and essayist Ralph Waldo Emerson on Algernon Swinburne

… with brass knobs on a gap-toothed and hoary ape, carried at first notice on the shoulder of Carlyle … who now in his dotage spits and chatters from a dirtier perch of his finding and fouling: coryphaeus or choragus of his Bulgarian tribe of autocoprophagous baboons, who make the filth they feed on.

Algernon Swinburne on both Emerson and Carlyle

For those of us without the dubious benefit of a classical education autocoprophagous means eating your own shit.

Scottish writer and essayist Thomas Carlyle

Perhaps the saddest lot that can befall a mortal man is to be the husband of a lady poet.

George Jean Nathan, American critic

He has occasional flashes of silence that make his conversation perfectly delightful.

British clergyman Sydney Smith on Thomas Babington Macaulay

Isn't it a shame that Maxwell Anderson's poetic licence has expired.

Noel Coward, British actor and dramatist

A woman once incessantly pestered English writer and lexicographer Samuel Johnson to read her play. Johnson told her that if she read it carefully herself, she'd find all the things he'd most likely ask her to correct.

'But sir,' she said, 'I have no time. I have already so many irons in the fire.'

'Well then, madam, the best thing that I can advise you is to put your tragedy along with your irons.'

His imagination resembles the wings of an ostrich.

Thomas Babington Macaulay on British writer John Dryden

Warren Harding, the only man, or woman, or child who ever wrote a simple declarative sentence with seven grammatical errors, is dead.

e.e. cummings, American poet

I do not hate the critics. I have nothing but compassion for them. How can I hate the crippled, the mentally deficient and the dead?

Albert Finney, British actor

Critics are just eunuchs at a gangbang.

George Burns, American comedian

A hack writer who would have been considered fourth rate in Europe, who tried out a few of the old proven 'sure-fire' literary skeletons with sufficient local colour to intrigue the superficial and the lazy.

William Faulkner on fellow American writer Mark Twain

Conrad spent a day finding the mot juste: then killed it.

Ford Madox Ford on fellow British writer Joseph Conrad

Addison was responsible for many of the evils from which English prose has since suffered. He made prose artful and whimsical, he made it sonorous when sonority was not needed, affected when it did not require affectation... He was the first Man of Letters. Addison had the misuse of an extensive vocabulary and so was able to invalidate a great number of words and expressions; the quality of his mind was inferior to the language which he used to express it.

British critic Cyril Connolly on British statesman and essayist Joseph Addison

God created the poet, then took a handful of the rubbish left over and made three critics.

T.J. Thomas

If you cannot get a job as a pianist in a brothel, you become a royal reporter.

Max Hastings, British journalist

Dear Randolph, utterly unspoilt by failure.

Noel Coward on Winston's son, writer Randolph Churchill

A triumph of modern science to find the only part of Randolph that wasn't malignant and remove it.

Evelyn Waugh on fellow British writer Randolph Churchill

Jackie Collins is to writing what her sister Joan is to acting.

Campbell Grison, critic

Gertrude Stein and me are just like brothers.

Ernest Hemingway, American writer

The essence of humour is surprise; that is why you laugh when you see a joke in *Punch*.

A.P. Herbert, British humorist

His ignorance was an Empire State Building of ignorance. You had to admire it for its size.

American journalist, writer and all-round wit Dorothy Parker on *New Yorker* editor Harold Ross

The Sun and *Mirror* have become the standard bearers of illiteracy.

Welsh novelist Emyr Humphreys on the British tabloids.

Barbara Cartland's eyes were twin miracles of mascara and looked like two small crows that had crashed into a chalk cliff.

Clive James, Australian writer

The fact that a man is a newspaper reporter is evidence of some flaw of character.

Lyndon B. Johnson, American president

Indeed, the freedom with which Dr Johnson condemns whatever he disapproves is astonishing.

Jane Welsh Carlyle, the 'Great Victorian Wife' of Thomas Carlyle

A woman who writes commits two sins; she increases the number of books and decreases the number of women.

Alphonse Kerr, Canadian politician

The trouble with Ian is that he gets off with women because he can't get on with them.

Rosamond Lehmann on fellow British novelist Ian Fleming

Drama critics are there to show gay actors what it is like to have a wife.

Hugh Leonard, Irish dramatist

British journalist and broadcaster Gilbert Harding was at a wedding when a fellow guest observed that the bride and groom made an ideal couple.

"You should know," Harding said. "You've slept with both of them."

Chuang Tzu was born in the fourth century BC. The publication of this book in English, over two thousand years after his death, is obviously premature.

Bernard Levin, British journalist

He is like someone on a quiz show who insists on giving answers in greater detail than is actually necessary.

Journalist William Leith on fellow Brit, the writer and composer Anthony Burgess

Anyone making love to Germaine Greer should have his guide dog confiscated and be awarded the Victoria Cross.

Bernard Manning, British comedian

His very frankness is falsity. In fact, it seems falser than his insincerity.

New Zealand author Katherine Mansfield on her husband John Middleton Murry

Tragedy is when I cut my little finger. Comedy is when you fall into an open sewer and die.

Mel Brooks, American film maker

Before they made S.J. Perlman, they broke the mould.

Groucho Marx, American actor and comedian

From the moment I picked your book up until I laid it down I was convulsed with laughter. Some day I intend reading it.

Groucho Marx, American actor and comedian

The triumph of sugar over diabetes.

American drama critic George Jean Nathan on the works of British writer J.M. Barrie

The conscientious Canadian critic is one who subscribes to the *New York Times* so that he knows at first hand what his opinions should be.

Eric Nichol, Canadian critic

A hyena that wrote poetry in tombs.

German philosopher Friedrich Nietzsche on the medieval Italian poet Dante Alighieri

Kingsley Amis once said that sex was a great cure for a hangover, which indeed must be the case, because if you thought Kingsley Amis was about to make love to you, you'd certainly avoid getting drunk in the first place.

Joseph O'Connor on his fellow British writer

Jane Austen's books, too, are absent from this library. Just that one omission alone would make a fairly good library out of a library that hadn't a book in it.

Mark Twain, American writer

One of the surest signs of Conrad's genius is that women dislike his works.

George Orwell on his fellow British writer

A huge pendulum attached to a small clock.

Russian critic Ivan Panin on British poet Samuel Taylor Coleridge

Take an idiot from a lunatic asylum and marry him to an idiot woman, and the fourth generation of the connection should be a good publisher from an American point of view.

Mark Twain, American writer

Hear no evil, see no evil and speak no evil—you'll never get a job working for a tabloid.

Phil Pastoret, British journalist

I would praise Joad's new book, but modesty forbids.

Bertrand Russell on fellow British philosopher C.E.M. Joad

Agate: My dear Lillian. I have long wanted to tell you that in my opinion you are the second-best actress in London.

Braithwaite: Thank you so much. I shall cherish that, coming from the second-best dramatic critic.

An exchange between American critic James Agate and British actress Lillian Braithwaite

'Mar-gott, how lovely to see you!'

'No, dear, the "t" is silent, as in "Harlow".

An exchange between Margot Asquith and actress Jean Harlow, who, out of ignorance, pronounced the 't' in Asquith's first name.

Only a flaw of nature prevented Vita Sackville-West from being one of nature's gentlemen.

Edith Sitwell, British poet

Reading Proust is like bathing in someone else's dirty water.

American critic Alexander Woollcott on the French writer

I do not think that Rousseau's poem *Ode to Posterity* will reach its destination.

Voltaire on his fellow French writer

Who can define him? His style is chaos illuminated by flashes of lightning. As a writer he has mastered everything except language; as a novelist he can do everything except tell a story. As an artist he is everything except articulate.

Oscar Wilde, Irish playwright and wit on British novelist George Meredith

There are two ways of disliking poetry. One is to dislike it. The other is to read Pope.

Oscar Wilde, Irish playwright and wit

You cannot hope to bribe or twist, thank God, the British journalist, but seeing what the man will do unbribed, there's no occasion to.

Humbert Woolf, British writer

I believe that I could write like Shakespeare, if I had a mind to try it.

William Wordsworth, British poet

Time is the only critic without ambition.

John Steinbeck, American writer

This film wasn't released. It escaped.

James Caan, American actor

The only trouble with Seamus O'Sullivan is that when he's not drunk he's sober.

W.B. Yeats on his fellow Irish poet

Being published by the Oxford University Press is rather like being married to a duchess; the honour is greater than the pleasure.

G.M. Young, British historian

There's no need for you to apologize at all. After all, I've never bored you half as much as you've bored me.

British actor and dramatist Noel Coward to British journalist Gilbert Harding who fell asleep during one of Coward's plays.

Her Victoria made me feel that Albert had married beneath his station.

Noel Coward, commenting on an actress playing the part of Queen Victoria

It is only an auctioneer who can equally and impartially admire all schools of art.

Oscar Wilde, Irish playwright and wit

Stages, Screens and Boxes

I suppose he looks all right, if your taste runs to septuagenarians with blow waves and funny stretch marks around the ears.

British journalist Lynn Barber on the American actor Kirk Douglas

In California, they don't throw their garbage away—they make it into TV shows.

Woody Allen, American film maker, comic and writer

Elizabeth Sitwell is like a high altar on the move.

Elizabeth Bowen, Anglo-Irish novelist

Getting the costumes right on *Cleopatra* was like polishing the fish knives on the *Titanic*.

Julian Barnes, American critic

I don't have ulcers. I give them.

Harry Cohn, American producer

The impact of the play was like the banging together of two damp dishcloths.

Brendan Behan, Irish dramatist

Peter O'Toole delivers every line with a monotonous tenor bark as if addressing an audience of deaf Eskimos.

Michael Billington, British drama critic

A day away from Tallulah Bankhead is like a month in the country.

Anonymous comment on the American actress

Bette and I are very good friends. There's nothing I wouldn't say to her face—both of them.

Tallulah Bankhead on Bette Davis

Mr Lorre's idea of playing a he-man was to extend his chest and then follow it slowly around stage.

Heywood Broun, American journalist

This film cost $31 million. With that I could have invaded some country.

Clint Eastwood, American actor and director

It's great to be with Bill Buckley, because you don't have to think. He takes a position and you automatically take the opposite one and you know you're right.

J.K. Galbraith, Canadian American economist

William F. Buckley looks and sounds not unlike Hitler—but without the charm.

American writer Gore Vidal on the politically conservative television personality

Anyone who lies about Gore Vidal is doing him a kindness.

William F. Buckley Jnr, American critic

With the collapse of vaudeville new talent has no place to stink.

George Burns, American comedian

British broadcaster Gilbert Harding was to interview American actress Mae West on the radio. During preparations Mae West's manager asked Harding to try to sound 'sexier' when he interviewed her. To which end Gilbert replied:

If, sir, I were endowed with the power of conveying unlimited sexual attraction through the potency of my voice, I would not be reduced to accepting a miserable pittance for the BBC for interviewing a faded female in a damp basement.

The best that can be said about Norwegian television is that it gives you the sensation of a coma without the worry and inconvenience.

Bill Bryson, American writer

Joan Collins unfortunately can't be with us tonight. She's busy attending the birth of her next husband.

John Parrott, British presenter

He directed rehearsals with the airy deftness of a rheumatic deacon producing Macbeth for a church social.

Noel Coward, British actor and dramatist

Most of it is so slowly paced you could not only pour yourself a drink between lines of dialogue, but add ice too.

Evening Standard on *Shaft's Big Score*

A first night audience consists of the unburied dead.

Orson Bean, British actor

Me no Leica.

Critic Caroline Lejeune on *I Am A Camera*

A.E. Matthews ambled his way through the play like a charming retriever who has buried a bone and can't quite remember where.

Noel Coward, British actor and dramatist

Edward Woodward—his name sounds like someone farting in the bath.

Noel Coward, British actor and dramatist

In Hollywood, writers are only considered the first drafts of human beings.

Frank Deford, American journalist

My favourite comedian is Frank Carson. Over the years I have enjoyed his joke very much.

Ken Dodd on a fellow British comedian

He played the king as if afraid that at any moment someone would play the ace.

American writer Eugene Field reviewing an actor's performance

Dear Ingrid Bergman—speaks five languages and can't act in any of them.

British actor John Gielgud on the Swedish-American actor

Barrett: You don't think that you are the only actor who can play Hamlet, do you?

Irving: Not at all. But you are the only actor who can't.

American actor Wilson Barrett response to Sir Henry Irving's questioning of his suitability to play *Hamlet* on the American stage.

Stages, Screens and Boxes

Some of the greatest love affairs I have known have involved one actor, unassisted.

Wilson Mizner, American playwright

Before television, people didn't know what a headache looked like.

D. Fields, American critic

He emits an air of overwhelming vanity combined with some unspecific nastiness, like a black widow spider in heat. But nobody seems to notice. He could be reciting 'Fox's Book of Martyrs' in Finnish and these people would be rolling out of their seats.

British playwright Roger Gellert on British comedian John Cleese

My dear chap! Good isn't the word!

British librettist W.S. Gilbert greeting an actor in his dressing room after a particularly bad performance.

A script of *Brideshead Revisited* needs an intravenous dose of syrup of figs or just a bullet.

A.A. Gill, British columnist

The plays of Samuel Beckett remind me of something Sir John Betjamen might do if you filled him up with Benzedrine and then force-fed him with Guinness intravenously.

Tom Davis, British journalist

You always knew where you were with Sam Goldwyn. Nowhere.

F. Scott Fitzgerald, American writer

It's greater than a masterpiece—why, it's mediocre!

Samuel Goldwyn, American film studio director

There is less to this than meets the eye.

American actor Tallulah Bankhead commenting on a play

Modesty is the artifice of actors, similar to passion in call girls.

Jackie Gleason, American comedian

Any picture in which Errol Flynn is the best actor is its own worst enemy.

Ernest Hemingway, American writer

He gives her class and she gives him sex.

Katharine Hepburn on fellow American actors Fred Astaire and Ginger Rogers

Having your book turned into a movie is like seeing your oxen turned into bouillon cubes.

John Le Carré, British author

It's a new low for actresses when you have to wonder what's between her ears instead of her legs.

Katherine Hepburn on fellow American actor Sharon Stone

Television is still in its infancy—that's why you have to get up and change it so often.

Michael Hynes, American journalist

Film directors are people too short to become actors.

Josh Greenfield, American journalist

After my act there was a lot of clapping and booing. But the clapping was for the booing.

Milton Berle, American comedian

His critiques of films are subtle and can be very amusing, especially the ones he hasn't seen.

British artist David Hockney on American film director Billy Wilder

My seventh film, *The Cool Mikado*, had the appearance of being made in a wind tunnel.

Frankie Howard, British comic actor

She knows when she should go on and she knows when she should go off—it's the bit in between that foxes her.

Hugh Hunt

As an actress, her only flare is in her nostrils.

Pauline Kael, American critic

Hook and Ladder is the sort of play that gives failure a bad name.

Walter Kerr, American critic

As in the outfitting of the *Titanic*, no expense has been spared on this production of *The Romans in Britain*.

Francis King, American critic

When it comes to acting, Joan Rivers has the range of a wart.

American critic Stewart Klein on the comedian

Here's where we get out the thesaurus and look up synonyms for 'garbage.'

American critic Mike LaSalle on the movie *Shanghai Knights*

During the rehearsals of Dorothy Parker's play *Close Harmony* the director was concerned about the jiggling large breasts of one of the leading ladies.

Director: Shouldn't she be wearing a bra?

Parker: Good God, no! At least something on the stage is moving.

Michael Caine can out-act any, well nearly any, telephone kiosk you care to mention.

Hugh Leonard, Irish dramatist

I cannot sing, dance or act—what else would I be but a talk show host.

David Letterman, American television presenter

The plot of *Who Killed Agatha Christie?* has as many holes as a sieve and is far less entertaining.

Bernard Levin, British journalist

In this production of *Macbeth*, the prompter stole the show.

Peter Lewis, American critic

For the eye, too much; for the ear, too little; for the mind, nothing at all.

British journalist Bernard Levin on Franco Zefirelli's *Othello*

Raquel Welch is silicone from the knees up.

Gorge Masters, American critic

I knew right away that Rock Hudson was gay when he did not fall in love with me.

Italian actor Gina Lollogrigida on the American actor Rock Hudson

I had a video made of my recent knee operation. The doctor said it was the best movie I ever starred in.

Shirley MacLaine, American actor

She is one of the few actresses in Hollywood history who looks more animated in still photographs than she does on the screen.

American radio pesenter Michael Medved on American actor Raquel Welch

Hollywood is a trip through a sewer in a glass-bottomed boat.

Wilson Mizner, American playwright

David Frost is the bubonic plagiarist.

Jonathan Miller on fellow British screenwriter and television presenter

We used to have actresses trying to become stars; now we have stars trying to become actresses.

Sir Laurence Olivier, British actor

I've spent several years in Hollywood, and I still think the movie heroes are in the audience.

Wilson Mizner, American playwright

Miss United Dairies herself.

British actor David Niven on American actor Jayne Mansfield who was famous for her impressive décolletage

Barbra Streisand looks like a cross between an aardvark and an albino rat surmounted by a platinum-coated horse bun.

Del Prete has as much charm as a broomstick with a smile painted on it.

Diane Keaton's acting is really a nervous breakdown in slow motion.

The only talent Doris Day possesses is that of being absolutely sanitary; her personality untouched by human emotions, her brow unclouded by human thought, her form unsmudged by the slightest evidence of femininity.

Sitting through this movie is like having someone at a fancy Parisian restaurant who neither speaks nor read French, read out stentoriously the entire long menu in his best Arkansas accent and occasionally interrupt himself to chortle at his cleverness.

You have to have a stomach for ugliness to endure Carol Kane—to say nothing of the zombie-like expressions she mistakes for acting.

Elizabeth Taylor has grown so ample that it has become necessary to dress her almost exclusively in a variety of ambulatory tents. On the few occasions when she does reveal her bosom (or part thereof), one breast (or part thereof) proves sufficient to traverse an entire wide-screen frame—diagonally.

John Simon, Serbian-American critic

I suspect that Beckett is a confidence trick perpetrated on the twentieth century by a theatre-hating God. He remains the only playwright in my experience capable of making forty minutes seem like an eternity and the wrong kind of eternity at that.

British critic Sheridan Morley on Irish playwright Samuel Beckett

One of those inexplicable farces which capture the hearts of countless London-goers, despite plots of appalling banality and dialogue that writers of cat-food commercials might well spurn.

British critic Sheridan Morley on *No Sex Please—We're British*

If you're not careful, I'll play this scene as you want it.

Claude Raines, American actor on being micro-managed by a director

Mosquitos see Elizabeth Taylor and shout 'Buffet!'

This year Elizabeth Taylor is wearing Orson Welles' designer jeans.

Elizabeth Taylor's so fat, she puts mayonnaise on an aspirin.

Joan Rivers, American comedian

Elizabeth Taylor married Larry Fortensky, a man younger than her first wedding dress.

A.A. Gill, British columnist

I knew Elizabeth Taylor when she didn't know where her next husband was coming from.

American actor Anne Baxter on her fellow actor

> Nature, not content with denying him the art of thinking, conferred on him the gift of writing.
>
> George Bernard Shaw, Irish dramatist and critic

Shaw is the spinster aunt of English literature.

Kenneth Tynan, British writer

He hasn't enough sense to bore assholes in wooden hobbyhorses.

American journalist Dorothy Parker on an anonymous Hollywood producer

Awards are like haemorrhoids; sooner or later every asshole gets some.

Frederic Raphael, Anglo-American screenwriter

She ran the gamut of emotion from A to B.

American journalist Dorothy Parker on one of Katherine Hepburn's performances

Working with Julie Andrews is like being hit over the head with a Valentine's card.

Christopher Plummer on his fellow British actor

When do you want me to do that little something for which you are paying me all this money?

British actor Ellen Terry to a director

Burt Reynolds sings like Dean Martin with adenoids and dances like a drunk killing cockroaches.

Canadian media personality John Barbour on the American actor

My movies are the kind they show in prisons and aeroplanes, because nobody can leave.

Burt Reynolds, American actor

When in doubt, ascribe all quotations to Bernard Shaw.

Nigel Rees, British writer and presenter

Go on writing plays, my boy. One of these days a London producer will go into his office and say to his secretary, 'Is there a play from Shaw this morning? And when she says 'No,' he will say, 'Well, then we'll have to start on the rubbish.' And that's your chance, my boy.

George Bernard Shaw, Irish dramatist and critic

They say Tom Mix rides as if he's part of the horse, but they don't say which part.

America playwright and screenwriter Robert Sherwood on the American movie cowboy

Acting on television is like being asked by the captain to entertain the passengers while the ship goes down.

Peter Ustinov, British comedian and actor

Johnny, keep it out of focus. I want to win the foreign picture award.

Television is a twenty-one inch prison. I'm delighted with it because it used to be that films were the lowest form of art. Now we have something to look down upon.

Billy Wilder, American film director

The Birthday Party was like a vintage Hitchcock thriller which has been edited by a cross-eyed studio janitor with a lawnmower.

American film maker Orson Welles on British playwright Harold Pinter's work

When you are alone with Max Beerbohn he takes off his face and reveals his mask.

Oscar Wilde, Irish playwright and wit

The Russians love Brooke Shields because her eyebrows remind them of Leonid Brezhnev.

Robin Williams, American actor and comedian

If this play lasts overnight it should not only be considered a long run but a revival too.

Alexander Woollcott, American critic

My reputation grows with every failure.

George Bernard Shaw, Irish dramatist and critic

Playing with Balls and Other Things

There's this interior linesman who's as big as a gorilla and as strong as a gorilla. If he was as smart as a gorilla, he'd be fine.

Sam Bailey, American coach

The English rugby team—I've seen better centres in a box of Black Magic.

Max Boyce, Welsh comedian

Gary Lineker is the Queen Mother of football.

James Christopher, AQ: please supply title/description

The ideal board of football directors should be made up of three men—two dead and one dying.

Tommy Doherty, Scottish footballer

Paul Ince with a big white bandage on his head was running around the field looking like a pint of Guinness.

Paul Gascoigne, British footballer

I never pray on a golf course. Actually, the Lord answers my prayers everywhere except on the course.

Billy Graham, American evangelist

The amateur rugby union player has an inalienable right to play like a pillock.

Dick Greenwood, British footballer

Pro basketball coaching is when you wake up in the morning and wish that your parents had never met.

Bill Fitch, American coach

Bobby Robson's natural expression is that of a man who fears that he might have left the gas on.

David Lacey, British sports writer

Tony Cascarino is the biggest waste of money since Madonna's father bought her pyjamas.

Frank Lauder, American writer

I resigned as a coach because of illness and fatigue. The fans were sick and tired of me.

John Ralston, American coach

Cricket is the only game that you can actually put on weight when playing.

Tommy Docherty, Scottish footabller

Football combines the worst features of American life—frantic violence punctuated by committee meetings.

George Will, American columnist

Ted Dexter was a master of placing both feet in his mouth at the same time.

Ian Botham, British cricketer

Hack Rowell had the acerbic wit of Dorothy Parker and, according to most New Zealanders, a similar knowledge of rugby.

Mark Reason, British sports writer on England's coach

Of course there should be women basketball referees. Incompetence should not be confined to one sex.

Bill Russell, American basketball player

Golf and sex are the only things that you can enjoy without being any good at them.

Jimmy Demaret, American golfer

Managing Dunfermline Athletic is a great job, except for the Saturday afternoons.

Jockey Scott, British football manager

Tommy Smith could start a riot in a graveyard.

Bill Shankly, Scottish football manager

Dear Lord, if there be cricket in heaven, let there also be rain.

Alec Douglas-Home, British politician

I am to cricket what Dame Sybil Thorndyke is to non-ferrous welding.

Frank Muir, British writer

Women playing cricket should treat it as a matter between consenting females in private.

Michael Parkinson, British television personality

I never play cricket. It requires one to assume such indecent postures.

Oscar Wilde, Irish playwright and wit

Michael Chang has all the fire and passion of a public service announcement, so much so that he makes Pete Sampras appear fascinating.

Alex Ramsay, American sports writer

Pancho Gonzales was the most even-tempered man I ever knew. Always mad.

Ben Thomas, Australian actor

If you want to take long walks, take long walks. If you want to hit things with a stick, hit things with a stick. But there's no excuse for combining the two and putting the results on TV. Golf is not so much a sport as an insult to lawns.

Dave Barry, American author and humorist

It's a marriage. If I had to choose between my wife and my putter—I'd miss her.

Gary Player, American golfer

Jack Nicklaus isn't really a golfer. He's just been on a thirty-year lucky streak.

Henry Beard, American humorist

My back swing off the first tee put the pro in mind of an elderly woman of dubious morals trying to struggle out of dress too tight around the shoulders.

Patrick Campbell, Irish journalist

Give me a man with big hands, big feet and no brains and I will make a golfer out of him.

Walter Hagen, American golfer

Golf is an ineffectual attempt to direct an uncontrollable sphere into an inaccessible hole with instruments ill adapted to the purpose.

Winston Churchill, British statesman

The reason the pro tells you to keep your head down is so you can't see him laughing.

Phyllis Diller, American comedian

Steve Ballesteros drives into territory Daniel Boone couldn't find.

Fuzzy Zoeller, American golfer

Colin Montgomerie is a few fries short of a Happy Meal. His mind goes on vacation and leaves his mouth in charge.

David Feherty, Irish golfer

A caddy is someone who accompanies the golfer and didn't see the ball either.

Joe Francis, American footballer

I owe everything to golf. Where else would a guy with an IQ like mine earn so much money?

Hubert Green, American golfer

Driving Mark McCormack's getaway car is the best job in golf.

George Low, American manager

Golf is so popular simply because it is the best game in the world at which to be bad.

A.A. Milne, British writer

Hubert Green swings like a drunk trying to find a keyhole in the dark.

Jim Murray, American sports writer

Gerald Ford doesn't realise he can't hit a ball through a tree trunk.

Jack Nicklaus on the American president's famous clumsiness

Gerald Ford made golf a contact sport.

The principle difference between Baba Zahanas and myself is that I hit the ball like a girl and she hits the ball like a man.

I once played a round with Jack Nicklaus and I asked him what most impressed him about my golf. 'Your score keeping,' he replied.

Arnold Palmer has won about as much money playing golf as I've paid on lessons.

Bob Hope, American comedian who was an enthusiastic rather than skilful golfer

I've seen better swings than Bob Hope's in a condemned playground.

American golfer Arnold Palmer on the comedian

Arnold Palmer turned golf into a game of 'Hit it hard, go find it and hit it hard again!'

John Schulian, American writer

Arnold Palmer would go for the flag from the middle of an alligator's back.

I'm not saying my game is bad at the moment, but if I grew tomatoes, they'd come up sliced.

My swing is so bad I look like a caveman killing his lunch.

No one who ever had lessons would have a swing like mine. If it wasn't for golf, I don't know what I'd be doing. If my I.Q. had been two points lower, I'd have been a tree somewhere.

Lee Trevino, American golfer

In the US first-class golfers take as long to choose a wife as a club. Sometimes they make the wrong choice in each case.

Dai Rees, British golfer

For most amateurs the best wood in the bag is the pencil.

Chi Chi Rodriguez, American golfer

It's hard to tell whether Americans have become such liars because of golf or income tax.

Will Rogers, American humorist

Golf is a game in which the ball lies poorly and the players well.

Art Rosenbaum, American artist

If a lot of people gripped a knife and fork like they do a golf club, they'd starve to death.

Sam Snead, American golfer

I'm using a new putter because the old one didn't float too well.

Craig Stadler, American golfer

Ocean racing is like standing under a cold shower tearing up five-pound notes.

Edward Heath, British politician

A fishing rod is a stick with a worm at one end and a fool at the other.

Samuel Johnson, English writer and lexicographer

There's a fine line between fishing and just standing on the shore like an idiot.

Steven Wright, American comedian

I've seen George Foreman shadow boxing and the shadow won.

Sonny Liston is so ugly that when he cries, the tears run down the back of his head.

Muhammad Ali, American boxer

Jack Dempsey hits like an epileptic pile driver.

Harry C. Witwert, American boxer

Playing with Balls and Other Things

Jake LaMotta and I fought six times. We almost got married.

Sugar Ray Robinson, American boxer

Rocky Marciano didn't know enough boxing to know what a feint was. He never tried to out-guess you. He just kept trying to knock your brains out.

Archie Moore, American boxer

Sure there have been injuries and deaths in boxing but none of them serious.

Alan Minter, British boxer

In the World Darts Championships in 1982, Jocky Wilson missed when attempting to shake hands with an opponent.

Craig Brown, satirist

Someone threw a petrol bomb at Alex Higgins once and he drank it.

Frank Carson, British comedian

I went to a fight the other night and a hockey game broke out.

Rodney Dangerfield, American comedian

Ice hockey is a form of disorderly conduct in which a score is kept.

Doug Larson, British racer

Bryant Gumbel's ego has applied for statehood. If it's accepted it will be the fifth largest.

American weather presenter Willard Scott on the sportscaster who spent 15 years anchoring the *Today* show.

Mountain climbers rope themselves together to prevent the sensible ones going home.

Earl Wilson, American journalist

Jogging is for people who aren't intelligent enough to watch breakfast television.

British comedian Victoria Wood

The only man who makes money following horses is the one who does it carrying a broom and shovel.

Elbert Hubbard, American writer

I am a jockey because I was too small to be a window cleaner and too big to be a garden gnome.

Adrian Maguire, Irish jockey

People say that sailing is an expensive sport, but to own a racehorse is the equivalent of burning a yacht on the front lawn every year.

Adam Nicholson, British writer

Smorgasbord of Insults

Do they ever shut up on your planet?

Don't go away. I want to forget you exactly as you are.

I refuse to star in your psychodrama.

I'm already visualizing the duct tape over your mouth.

I'd like to leave you with this thought: If I've said anything to insult you, I've tried my utmost—believe me.

Learn from your parents' mistakes. Use birth control!

Let's go some place were we can each be alone.

May I have the pleasure of your absence?

Next time you give your clothes away, stay in them.

Save your breath. You'll need it to blow up your date.

The more I think of you, the less I think of you.

Slit your wrists, it will lower your blood pressure.

The only thing your conversation needs is a little lockjaw.

The sooner I never see you again, the better it'll be for both of us when we meet.

You're about as useful as a chocolate teapot.

You're someone who would make a perfect stranger. Start being one now.

First left, go along the corridor. You'll see a door marked Gentlemen, but don't let that deter you.

Anonymous

He was the sort of man who would throw a drowning man both ends of a rope.

Arthur Baer, American boxer

If only these old walls could talk, how boring they would be.

Robert Benchley, American humorist

His mind is so open that the wind whistles through it.

Heywood Broun, American journalist

He knew everything about literature except how to enjoy it.

Joseph Heller, American novelist

All modern men are descended from wormlike creatures, but it shows more on some people.

Will Cuppy, American humorist

Yeah, she's beautiful, but you can't find her IQ with a flashlight.

From *The Greatest American Hero*

To call him grey would be an insult to porridge.

Nicholas Fairburn on Scottish judge Lord Hope

Behrman—forgotten but not gone.

George S. Kaufman on the fellow American playwright who would outlive him by 12 years

Such time as he can spare from the adornment of his person he devotes to the neglect of his duties.

Samuel Johnson, English writer and lexicographer

Some cause happiness wherever they go; others whenever they go.

Oscar Wilde, Irish playwright and wit

I am free of all prejudice. I hate everyone equally.

W.C. Fields, American actor

I have been friendly with Brendan Behan only in the hope that I would be free from the horror of his acquaintanceship.

British writer Patrick Kavanaugh on the Irish dramatist

He looked at me as if I was a side dish he hadn't ordered.

Ring Lardner, American sports columnist

Egotism is the anaesthetic that dulls the pain of stupidity.

Frank Leahy, American football coach

Talking to Francis gave me the sensation of settling slowly to the bottom of the ocean.

Scout Finch in Harper Lee's *To Kill a Mockingbird*

I am going to memorise your name and throw my head away.

Oscar Levant, American musician and wit

Under my flabby exterior lies an enormous lack of character.

Oscar Levant, American musician and wit

You're taking psychology? Are you like the example for the class or something?

Natalie Mark, American comedian

Don't look now, but there's one too many in this room and I think it's you.

Groucho Marx, American actor and comedian

I regard you with an indifference bordering on aversion.

Robert Louis Stevenson, Scottish writer

I would not want to put him in charge of snake control in Ireland.

American politician Eugene McCarthy on an anonymous rival. [Note: Ireland has no snakes].

Failure has gone to his head.

Wilson Mizner, American playwright

He knows so little and knows it so fluently.

Ellen Glasgow, American writer

He had almost every quality you could wish to have, except that he had the average brain of an average English gentleman. He lacked that little extra cubic centimetre which produces genius.

British admiral and statesman Louis Mountbatten on Earl Alexander of Tunis

Why don't you bore a hole in yourself and let the sap run out?

Groucho Marx, American actor and comedian

He was humble for a fortnight, but nobody noticed.

Katherine Whitehorn, British journalist

He was a self-made man who owed his lack of success to nobody.

Joseph Heller, American writer

His bounty and generosity always creates more horses asses' than there are horses to attach them to.

Thomas Perry, American writer

From the silence that prevails I conclude that Lauderdale has been telling a joke.

Richard Brinsley Sheridan, British playwright

Some folks are wise and some are otherwise.

Tobias George Smollett, Scottish writer

I could dance with you until the cows come home. On second thought I'd rather dance with the cows until you come home.

Groucho Marx, American actor and comedian

He is an old bore. Even the grave yawns for him.

Herbert Beerbohm Tree, British actor

British painter William Morris spent a lot of time in the various restaurants in the Eiffel Tower, so much so that one day one of the waiters said to him: 'You're obviously impressed with the tower, monsieur.' To which Morris replied:

Impressed? The only reason I'm in here is that it's the one place in Paris where I can avoid seeing this damned thing.

Get the facts straight first and then you can distort them as much as you please.

He is useless on top of the ground; he aught to be under it, inspiring the cabbages.

He was a solemn, unsmiling, sanctimonious old iceberg who looked like he was waiting for a vacancy in the Trinity.

His ignorance covers the world like a blanket, and there's scarcely a hole in it anywhere.

I could never learn to like her, except on a raft at sea with no other provisions in sight.

Why do you sit there looking like an envelope without any address on it?

Mark Twain, American writer

He is so mean, he won't let his little baby have more than one measle at a time.

Eugene Field, American writer

He was trying to save both his faces.

John Gunther, American journalist

He is a fine friend. He stabs you in the front.

Leonard Louis Levinson, American humorist

A healthy male adult bore consumes each year one and a half times his own weight in other people's patience.

John Updike, American novelist

What were you when you were alive?

Henny Youngman, American comedian

An extraordinary man! There's only one art he doesn't understand—the art of dialogue.

Voltaire's comment after being subjected to Denis Diderot's incessant monologue

It is said of Sarah, Duchess of Marlborough, that she never put dots over her 'i's, to save ink.

Horace Walpole, British writer

He looked as inconspicuous as a tarantula on a slice of angel food.

Raymond Chandler, American writer

Why be disagreeable, when with a little effort you can be impossible.

Douglas Woodruff, British editor

No shirt is too young to be stuffed.

Larry Zolf on fellow Canadian politician Joe Clark

An exchange between a pompous and self-absorbed young man and British politician John Wilkes:

Young man: I was born between twelve and one o'clock on 1st January. Isn't that strange?

Wilkes: No not at all. You could only have been conceived on 1st April.

I think he's the most over-rated human being since Judas Iscariot won the AD 31 Best Disciple Competition.

If your parents got a divorce would they still be brother and sister?

You're obviously from the shallow end of the gene pool.

You're like one of those 'idiot savants,' except without the 'savant' part.

Anonymous

She tells enough white lies to ice a wedding cake.
British aristocrat and socialite Margot Asquith

He is like a mule, with neither pride of ancestry nor hope of progeny.
Robert G. Ingersoll

At his most detestable, he was no hypocrite, but rather his own worst enemy, prey to a moral blindness which was instinctive rather than reasoned. How he would have hated himself had he been able to view some of his acts objectively...
American writer Kenneth W. Porter on capitalist John Jacob Astor

He hasn't a single redeeming vice.
Oscar Wilde, Irish playwright and wit

He had all the virtues I dislike and none of the vices I admire.
Winston Churchill, British prime minister

He has not one single redeeming defect.
Benjamin Disraeli on fellow British prime minister William Gladstone

She was like a sinking ship firing on the rescuers.

Alexander Woollcott, American critic

He is as good as his word—and his word is no good.

Seamus MacManus, Irish humorist

He must have killed a lot of men to have made so much money.

Moliere, French playwright

What has a tiny brain, a big mouth, and an opinion nobody cares about? You!

From the television sitcom *Murphy Brown*

A wit with dunces, and a dunce with wits.

Alexander Pope on a fellow British writer

He's the only man I ever knew who had rubber pockets so he could steal soup.

You're a mouse studying to be a rat.

Wilson Mizner, American playwright

He was so crooked, you could have used his spine for a safety pin.

Dorothy L. Sayers, British writer

It's a pity that Marie Stope's mother had not thought of birth control.

Muriel Spark, Scottish writer

An exchange between George Bernard Shaw and a fellow guest at a dinner party. He asked the lady if she would go to bed with a man for five hundred pounds.

Guest: That would depend on how good-looking he was.

Shaw: Would you do it for ten bob then?

Guest: What do you take me for?

Shaw: We have already settled that. All we are now doing is agreeing on the price.

On another occasion a society hostess invited Shaw to a dinner stating that she would be 'at home' on a certain date.

'G.B.S also,' he replied.

Shaw couldn't even be nice to people who paid him a compliment. A particularly beautiful woman once suggested that they have a child together.

'Imagine a child with my body and your brain!' she said.

'Yes, but what if it had my body and your brain?' he countered.

You take the lies out of him, and he'll shrink to the size of your hat; you take the malice out of him, and he'll disappear.
Mark Twain, American writer

The food was so tasteless you could eat a meal of it and belch and not be reminded of anything.
Red Foxx, American comedian

He is alive, but only in the sense that he cannot be legally buried.
Geoffrey Madan

I know of nothing more despicable and pathetic than a man who devotes all of the hours of the waking day to the making of money for money's sake.

American oil baron and billionaire John D. Rockefeller, who did in fact seem to spend every waking moment making money.

It would have been twice as bad if they had sent the dog.

British prime minister Harold MacMillan commenting on the huge crowds in London gathered to honour the first man in space Yuri Gagarin.

Visitors: Good morning, we are Jehovah's witnesses.

George Bernard Shaw: Good morning. I'm Jehovah. How are we doing?

I've had a perfectly wonderful evening. But this wasn't it.

Groucho Marx, American actor and comedian

If only he'd wash his neck, I'd wring it.

British academic John Sparrow on a colleague

Poor old Mortlake, who had only two topics of conversation, his gout and his wife. I never could quite make out which of the two he was talking about.

Oscar Wilde, Irish playwright and wit

Exchange between Winston Churchill, who fell asleep on a train with his flies undone, and a female passenger who enters his compartment.

Passenger: Sir! Your penis is sticking out!

Churchill: Madam, you flatter yourself. It is merely hanging out.

An exchange between British actress Beatrice Lillie and an anonymous woman at a dinner table. The woman asked Lillie if the pearls on her necklace were real. When Lillie replied 'yes', the woman reached across the table, grabbed the pearls and tried to run them across her teeth.

Woman: The pearls are not real! They're cultured.

Lillie: How would you know, with false teeth?

He was a bit like a corkscrew. Twisted, cold and sharp.

Kate Cruise O'Brien, Irish writer

The Wisdom of Bumpers

I used to be schizophrenic, but we're OK now. Allow me to introduce my selves.

A day without sunshine is like night.

A journey of a thousand miles begins with a cash advance.

Above all else, sky.

Adjure obfuscation.

Alcohol and calculus don't mix. DON'T DRINK AND DERIVE!

All I ask is the chance to prove that money can't make me happy.

All men are idiots, and I married their King.

Always Avoid Alliteration.

An Apple a day keeps Windows away.

Anything not worth doing is not worth doing well.

As long as there are tests, there will be prayer in public schools.

Beauty is in the eye of the beer holder.

Beer doesn't make you fat. It makes you lean (against doors, tables, walls).

Beer: It's not just for breakfast anymore.

Being 'over the hill' is much better than being under it!

Come to the dark side—we have cookies.

Consciousness: That annoying time between naps.

Constipation causes people not to give a crap.

Does anal-retentive have a hyphen?

Don't believe everything you think.

Don't treat me any differently than you would the Queen.

Double your drive space. Delete Windows.

Driver carries no cash. He's married.

Dyslexics Untie!

EARTH FIRST! We'll strip-mine the other planets later.

Ever stop to think, and forget to start again?

Every time you open your mouth, some idiot starts talking.

Excess is never too much in moderation.

First National Bank of Dad; Sorry, closed.

First things first; but not necessarily in that order.

Fishermen don't die; they just smell that way.

Forget world peace; visualize using your turn signal.

Getting on your feet means getting off your butt.

Give a person a fish and you feed them for a day; teach a person to use the Internet and they won't bother you for weeks.

God is my co-pilot, but the Devil is my bombardier.

God made us sisters; Prozac made us friends.

Hard work has a future payoff. Laziness pays off now.

I can't remember if I'm the good twin or the evil one.

I didn't believe in reincarnation in my last life, either!

I didn't climb to the top of the food chain to become a vegetarian!

I don't have a beer gut, I have a protective covering for my rock hard abs.

I don't have a license to kill. I have a learner's permit.

I don't think, therefore I am not.

I doubt, therefore I might be.

I feel better after I wine a little.

I fish, therefore I lie.

I had the right to remain silent, but I didn't have the ability.

I have the body of a god. Buddha.

I just want revenge. Is that so wrong?

I love animals. They're delicious.

I need someone real bad. Are you real bad?

I plan to live forever. So far, so good!

I said 'No' to drugs, but they didn't listen.

I thought I was indecisive; now I'm not so sure.

I took an IQ test and the results were negative.

I used to have a handle on life, but it broke.

I'm Not with Stupid Anymore.

If at first you don't succeed, call it version 1.0!

If I get you advantage, can I take drunk of you?

If it ain't broke, take it apart and fix it.

If it isn't broken, fix it until it is.

If it's not one thing, it's your mother.

If today were a fish I'd throw it back

If you are what you eat, I'm fast, cheap and easy.

If you believe in telepathy, think about honking.

If you can read this, I can hit my brakes and sue you.

If you can read this, I've lost the trailer!

If you can read this, you're not the president.

If you can't read this, thank the teacher's union.

If you observe this vehicle being operated in an unsafe manner, please try to think of it as one more anomaly in the cosmic order.

If you're happy and you know it see a shrink.

If you're not part of the solution, you're part of the precipitate.

I'm going to graduate on time, no matter how long it takes.

I'm not crazy, I've just been in a very bad mood for 30 years.

I'm not tense, just terribly, terribly alert.

I'm out of oestrogen and I've got a gun!

I'm pink, therefore I'm SPAM.

I'm still a hot babe, but now it comes in flashes.

I'm supposed to back up my hard drive, but how do I put it into reverse?

In America, anyone can be president. That's one of the risks you take.

IRS: Be The Audit You Can Be

Is it time for your medication or mine?

It's lonely at the top, but you eat better.

I've heard about the evils of drinking beer, so I gave up reading.

Jesus loves you! Everybody else thinks you're a jerk.

Jesus loves you! But I'm one of his favourites.

Just say 'NO' to negativity.

Karaoke bars combine two of the nation's greatest evils: people who shouldn't drink with people who shouldn't sing.

Keep honking while I reload.

Kids in the back seat cause accidents; Accidents in the back seat cause kids.

Knowledge is power, and power corrupts. So study hard and be evil.

Lawyers have feelings too (allegedly).

Let's skip the insults and get right down to your butt kicking!

Life is short. So buy the shoes!

Life would be easier if I had the source code.

Love may be blind, but marriage is a real eye opener.

Madness takes its toll. Please have exact change.

Money is the root of all evil. For more information, send $10 to me.

My drinking team has a bowling problem.

My feminine side is lesbian.

My mind is like a steel trap—rusty and illegal in most states.

My mood ring says back off

My mother is a travel agent for guilt trips.

My mother was a moonshiner, and I love her still.

My wife keeps complaining I never listen to her (or something like that).

My wife says I should get up and go to work, but the voices in my head say I should stay home and clean my guns.

Nebraska: At least the cows are sane.

Never believe generalizations.

Never knock on Death's door. Ring the bell and run, he hates that.

Never miss a good opportunity to shut up.

New Mexico: Cleaner than regular Mexico.

Nuke the Whales! We'll hunt them at night.

Quoting one is plagiarism. Quoting many is research.

Therapy is expensive. Popping bubble wrap is cheap. You choose.

Of all the things I've lost, I miss my mind the most.

Old age comes at a bad time.

On the journey of life, I choose the psycho path.

On your mark, get set, go away!

Out of my mind—back in five minutes.

People like you are the reason people like me need medication.

Practice safe lunch: Use a condiment.

Procrastinate now.

Reality is a crutch for people who can't handle drugs.

Rehab is for quitters.

Resistance is futile (if > 1 ohm).

Rock is dead. Long live paper and scissors.

Save the trees, wipe your butt with an owl.

Save the whales! Trade them for valuable prizes.

Say 'NO' to drugs. That will bring the prices down.

Screw world peace, visualize DRIVING.

Senior Citizen: Give me my damn discount!

Smile, it's the second best thing you can do with your lips.

So many cats, so few recipes.

So many stupid people, and so few asteroids.

So you're a feminist. Isn't that cute?

Some days it's just not worth gnawing through the leather straps.

Some people are only alive because it is illegal to shoot them.

Sorry if I look interested, I'm not!

Stable relationships are for horses.

Stop repeat offenders. Don't re-elect them!

Stoplights timed for 30 mph are also timed for 60 mph.

Stress is when you wake up screaming and you realize you weren't asleep.

Suburbia: Where they tear out the trees and name streets after them.

That's not a haircut, it's a cry for help.

The bigger the hat, the better the cowboy.

The box said Windows 2000 or better. So I installed Linux.

The control key on the keyboard does not work.

The generation of random numbers is too important to leave to chance.

The last thing I want to do is hurt you. But it's still on the list.

The last time politics and religion were mixed, people were burned at the stake.

The meek shall inherit the earth—after we're through with it.

The Moral Majority is neither.

The more you complain the longer God makes you live.

The original point and click interface was a Smith & Wesson.

The trouble with the gene pool is that there's no lifeguard.

There are 10 types of people in the world. Those who understand binary, and those who don't.

Think globally, act galactically.

This bumper sticker intentionally left blank.

If you want breakfast in bed, sleep in the kitchen.

To err is human, to blame it on somebody else shows management.

Use the best: Linux for servers, Mac for graphics, Windows for solitaire.

Vegetarian: Indian word for lousy hunter.

Veni, Vidi, Velcro. I came, I saw, I stuck around.

Veni, Vedi, Visa: I Came, I Saw, I did a little shopping.

Wanted: Meaningful overnight relationship.

Warning: Dates on calendar are closer than they appear.

Watch out for the idiot behind me.

What we need is a patch for stupidity!

Well, at least the war on the environment is going well.

Well, this day was a total waste of makeup.

What if the hokey pokey is really what it's all about?

Whatever kind of look you were going for, you missed.

When I want your opinion, I'll beat it out of you.

Whenever I feel blue, I start breathing again.

When you do a good deed, get a receipt in case heaven is like the IRS.

Where there's a will, I want to be in it.

Who are these children, and why do they keep calling me Mom?

Without geometry, life is pointless.

Without ME, it's just AWESO.

Women who seek to be equal with men lack ambition.

Worry. God knows all about you.

WWJD (Who Wants Jelly Donuts?)

Wrinkled was not one of the things I wanted to be when I grew up!

You—off my planet.

You say I'm a bitch like it's a bad thing.

Your body would look good in my trunk.

You're just jealous because the voices only talk to ME.

Father Machine and Mother Nature

Scientists have discovered the noise made just prior to the Big Bang, which sounds something like 'oops.'

Cully Abrell (James Clayton), American screenwriter

If everyone on Earth stopped breathing for just an hour, the greenhouse effect would no longer be a problem.

Jerry Adler, American actor

Chaos Theory is a new theory invented by scientists panicked by the thought that the public were beginning to understand the old ones.

Virtual reality is a cutting-edge computer science project in which companies are investing millions of dollars in a frenzied attempt to reproduce an effect which can currently be achieved simply by looking out the window.

Mike Barfield, American musician

What is algebra exactly? Is it one of those three cornered things?

J.M. Barrie, Scottish novelist

The ants set an example to us all, but it is not a good one.

Max Beerbohm, British caricaturist

Monkeys and apes have the ability to speak but keep silent to avoid being put to work.

René Descartes, French mathematician

To err is human, but to really foul things up you need a computer.

Paul Ehrlich, German immunologist

Quod erat demonstrandum is Latin for, 'Don't argue with ME, you bastard.'

Russell Bell, American actor

The Internet is so big, powerful and pointless that for some people it is a complete substitute for life.

Andrew Brown, British computer acientist

Automatic simply means that you cannot repair it yourself.

Frank Capra, Italian-American Director

Weather forecast for tonight: dark.

George Carlin, American comedian

The best way to accelerate a Macintosh is at 9.8 metres per second.

Marcus Dolengo [Note: for those who forgot their high school science, 9.8 m/s is the acceleration due to gravity].

If ants are such busy workers, how come they find the time to go to all the picnics?

Marie Dressler, American actor

A computer is like an Old Testament God, with a lot of rules and no mercy.

Joseph Campbell, American mythologist

The two most abundant things in the universe are hydrogen and stupidity.

Harlan Ellison, American author

My dog understands every word I say but ignores it.

Michael Green, British theologian

The smallest hole will eventually empty the largest container, unless it is made intentionally for drainage, in which case it will clog.

Dave Grissom, American musician

The perfect computer has already been developed. You just feed in your problems and they never come out again.

Al Goodman, American musician

In ancient times they had no statistics so they had to fall back on lies.

Stephen Leacock, Canadian economist

You ask me if I keep a notebook in which to record my great ideas. I've only ever had one.

Only two things are infinite—the universe and human stupidity and I'm not sure about the former.

Albert Einstein, German physicist

A bishop wrote gravely to the *Times* inviting all nations to destroy 'the formula' for the atomic bomb. There is no simple remedy for ignorance so abysmal.

Peter Medaway, British journalist

The trouble with the Internet is that it is replacing masturbation as a leisure activity.

Patrick Murray, British actor

The most overlooked advantage to owning a computer is that if they foul up there's no law against whacking them around a little.

Eric Porterfield, British writer

Have you ever smelled a rain forest? They stink. They stink worse than a 13-year-old's bedroom.

A.A. Gill, British columnist

The best thing about the rain forests is that they never suffer from drought.

Dan Quayle, American Vice-President

Sex is just the mathematics urge sublimated.

M.C. Reed, British mathematician

82% of statistics are made up on the spot.

Vic Reeves, British comedian

Well, if I called the wrong number, why did you answer the phone?

James Thurber, American cartoonist

The Internet is like a herd of performing elephants with diarrhoea—massive, difficult to redirect, awe-inspiring, entertaining and a source of mind-boggling amounts of excrement when you least expect it.

Gene Spafford, American computer scientist

If builders built buildings the way computer programmers write programs, the first woodpecker that came along would destroy civilization.

Reede Stockton, American writer

Many snakes are actually quite short if you don't count the tail.

John Thompson, American sportsman

To you I'm an atheist. To God, I'm the loyal opposition.

As the poet said, 'Only God can make a tree,' probably because it's so hard to figure out how to get the bark on.

Eternal nothingness is fine if you happen to be dressed for it.

Woody Allen, American film maker, comic and writer

Mathematics was always my bad subject. I couldn't convince my teachers that many of my answers were meant ironically.

Calvin Trillin, American journalist

The only reason we had a son was to get someone to work the video. For ten years we used it as a night light.

Adrian Walsh, British comedian

God and Other Imponderables

A survey revealed that 96% of Americans believe in a God. 90% pray regularly. 71% believe in an afterlife and 41% attend church once a week. Another poll found that 3% believe they are God.

James Adams, American theologian

Being a Catholic doesn't stop you from sinning. It just stops you from enjoying it.

Cleveland Amory, American writer

Methodism is not really a religion. It's just a sort of insurance policy in case there turns out not to be a God.

Peter Barr, Australian barrister

A Christian is one who believes that the New Testament is a divinely inspired book, admirably suited to the spiritual needs of his neighbours.

Ambrose Bierce, American writer

What a pity that Noah and his party didn't miss the boat.

Mark Twain, American writer

He stopped sinning suddenly. He died.

Elbert Hubbard, American writer

A Calvinistic Presbyterian believes that all Catholics will be damned because they are predestined to be damned; an ordinary Presbyterian believes that all Catholics will be damned on their merits.

John Bartley, American cinematographer

His was the sort of career that made the Recording Angel think seriously about taking shorthand.

Nicholas Bentley, British writer

I know God will not give me anything I cannot handle. I just wish he didn't trust me so much.

Albanian Nun Mother Teresa

God made everything out of nothing. But the nothingness shows through.

Paul Valéry, French essayist

It is the function of vice to keep virtue within reasonable bounds.

British writer Samuel Butler

If Dorothy Johnson doesn't know as much as God, she most certainly knows as much as He did at her age.

Ilka Chase, American actor

The one thing father always gave up for Lent was going to church.

Clarence Day, American writer

If absolute power corrupts absolutely, where does that leave God?

George Deacon, British oceanographer

A 62-year-old friend of mine went to bed at night and prayed, 'Please, God, give me skin like a teenager's.' Next day, she woke up with acne.

Phyllis Diller, American comedian

It is no accident that the symbol of a bishop is a crook and the symbol of an archbishop is a double-cross.

Gregory Dix, British monk

Almost all religions agree that God is fond of music, sometimes dancing and always of processions.

Robert Morely, British actor

More people have been driven insane through religious hysteria than by drinking alcohol.

The average minister should be unfrocked immediately and prevented, by force if necessary, from communicating any ideas to persons under 35.

W.C. Fields, American actor

An Anglican clergyman is invisible 6 days a week and incomprehensible on the 7th.

Dean Inge, British clergyman

Lutherans are like Scottish people, only with less frivolity.

Garrison Keillor, American humorist

God and Other Imponderables

The most scandalous charges against the Pope were suppressed. His Holiness was accused only of piracy, rape, murder, sodomy and incest.

Edward Gibbon on Pope John XXII

Only a vegan nun who has taken a vow of silence lives without hurting anyone.

Tim Rayment, British journalist

There are three sorts of country parson in my diocese. Those who have gone out of their minds. Those who are going out of their minds. And those who have no minds to go out of.

Edward King, British cleric

Woody Allen has the sort of face that convinces you that God is a cartoonist.

Jack Kroll, American critic

Lest O Lord this prayer be too obscure, permit thy servant to illustrate it with an anecdote.

Allan Laing, British magistrate

Walking in a churchyard I have often asked myself, 'Where are all the bad people buried?'

Charles Lamb, English essayist

I am half-Catholic and half-Jewish. When I go to confession, I bring my lawyer with me.

Ed Mann, American dramatist

The good Lord never gives you more than you can handle—unless you die of something.

Steve Martin, American comedian

Metaphysics is an attempt to prove the incredible by an appeal to the unintelligible.

H.L. Mencken, American journalist and political commentator

Almost all religions agree that God is fond of music, sometimes dancing and always of processions.

Robert Morely, British actor

Sixty minutes of thinking of any kind is bound to lead to confusion and unhappiness.

James Thurber, American cartoonist

There is nothing so stupid as an educated man, if you get him off the thing he was educated in.

Will Rogers, American humorist

I once asked a man what he thought would happen to him after he died. He replied that he believed he would inherit eternal bliss, but didn't want to talk about such unpleasant subjects.

F.W. Myers, American businessman

One goldfish told another that he intended to become an atheist. 'Don't be crazy,' the other goldfish replied. 'Of course there's a God. Who do you think changes the water every day?'

Richard Needham, British politician

God and Other Imponderables

I'd love to see Christ come back to crush the spirit of hate and make men put down their guns. I'd also like just one more hit single.

Tiny Tim, American musician

If I ever come face to face with my maker I shall say 'God why did you make the evidence for your existence so insufficient?'

Bertrand Russell, British economist

I have to believe in the Apostolic Succession. There is no other way of explaining the descent of the Bishop of Exeter from Judas Iscariot.

Sydney Smith, British cleryman

In the beginning there was nothing and God said, 'Let there be light!' and there was still nothing, but everyone could see it.

Dave Thomas

Every human being commits 630,720,000 sins by the age of 30.

Augustus Toplady, Anglican clergyman

The primary function of a priest is to keep his congregation awake.

Peter Ustinov, British comedian and actor

You have no idea how much nastier I would be if I were not a Catholic. Without supernatural aid I would hardly be a human being.

Evelyn Waugh, British writer

I admire the Pope. I have a lot of respect for anyone who can tour without an album.

Rita Rudner, American comedian

Sailors ought never to go to church. They ought to go to hell, where it is much more comfortable.

H.G. Wells, British writer

I don't know if God exists, but it would be better for his reputation if he didn't.

Jules Renard, Fench writer

I read The Book of Job last night. I don't think that God comes well out of it.

Virginia Woolf, British author

One half of the world does not believe in God, and the other half does not believe in me.

Oscar Wilde, Irish playwright and wit

The Trials of Life

Our family was so poor we used to go to Kentucky Fried Chicken and lick other people's fingers.

Lenny Banks, American humorist

Our terraced house was so small the mice walked about on their hind legs.

Les Dawson, British comedian

Blood is thicker than water and much more difficult to get out of the carpet.

What if everything is an illusion and nothing exists? In that case, I definitely overpaid for my carpet.

I don't want to achieve immortality through my work, I want to achieve it through not dying.

Woody Allen, American film maker, comic and writer

Most human problems can be solved by an appropriate charge of high explosive.

Blaster Bates, British demolitionist

A Freudian slip is when you say one thing when you're really thinking about a mother.

Cliff Claven, American humorist

The secret of creativity is knowing how to hide your sources.

Albert Einstein, German physicist

We must believe in luck, for how else can we explain the success of those we don't like?

Jean Cocteau, French film-maker

They tell you that you'll lose your mind when you grow older. What they don't tell you is that you won't miss it very much.

Malcolm Crowley

The secret of creativity is knowing how to hide your sources.

Albert Einstein, German physicist

Have you ever been in therapy? No? You should try it. It's like a really easy game show where the correct answer to every question is: 'Because of my mother'.

Robin Greenspan, American actor

I performed badly in the Civil Service examinations because evidently I knew more about economics than my examiners.

J.M. Keynes, British Economist

Juries scare me. I don't want to put my faith in people who weren't smart enough to get out of jury duty.

Monica Piper

When guests stay too long, treat them like the rest of the family. If they don't leave then, they never will.

Martin Ragaway, American screenwriter

Laziness is nothing more than the habit of resting before you get tired.

Jules Renard, French writer

The efficacy of our criminal jury system is marred only by the difficulty of finding twelve men every day who do not know anything and cannot read.

Mark Twain, American writer

This year one third of the nation will be ill-nourished, ill-housed and ill-clad. Only they call it summer vacation.

Joseph Salak, American writer

If God had intended us to fly, he would have made it easier to get to the airport.

Jonathan Winters, American comedian

You know when you put a stick in the water and it looks like it's bent but it really isn't? That's why I don't take baths.

Steven Wright, American comedian

Making a Dying

Life is anything that dies when you stamp on it.

Dave Barry, American author and humorist

Epitaph for a Hollywood actress: She Sleeps Alone At Last.

Robert Benchley, American humorist

Everyone seems to fear dying alone and I have never understood this point of view. Who wants to die and be polite at the same time?

Quentin Crisp, British writer and 'Great Stately British Homo'

The great comfort of turning 49 is the realisation that you are now too old to die young.

Paul Dickson

I laid my wife
Beneath this stone
For her repose
And for my own

Chief Ottawa, American tribal chief

If you're killed, you've lost a very important part of your life.

Brooke Shields, American actress

Life is anything that dies when you stamp on it.

Dave Barry, American author and humorist

I'm not afraid to die. I just don't want to be there when it happens.

I have a fear that there is an afterlife but no one will know where it's being held.

Woody Allen, American film maker, comic and writer

If ghosts can walk through walls, how come they don't fall through the floor?

Steven Wright, American comedian

If this is dying, then I don't think much of it.

British writer Lytton Strachey, who died on 31 January 1931 from the effects of undiagnosed stomach cancer.